CAREERS IN
MUSIC

Mark Edgley Smith
and Ruth Yockney

**KOGAN
PAGE**

First published in 1999

Kogan Page Limited
120 Pentonville Road
London N1 9JN

© Kogan Page, 1999

Acknowledgements

Many people aided us in the writing of this book by giving us the benefit of their knowledge and experience: our grateful thanks to all of them. We're particularly indebted to those who agreed to act as case studies and exerted themselves in interview to give helpful answers to our sometimes unhelpful questions.

MES
RY

British Library Cataloguing in Publication Data

A CIP record for this book is available from the British Library.

ISBN 0 7494 2957 7

Typeset by Kogan Page Ltd
Printed and bound in Great Britain by Clays Ltd, St Ives plc

Contents

6. Where to study 58

Choosing the right course: the first step to success;
Music degrees; Specialized courses

7. Useful addresses 69

8. Useful publications 76

Books; Fact sheets published by the Incorporated
Society of Musicians, London; Newspapers and
periodicals

Introduction

Is this the Job for You?

Music first and foremost...

- ☐ Are you sure you want a career as a professional musician?
- ☐ Are you good at making contacts and seizing opportunities?
- ☐ Are you prepared to work long and unsociable hours (in rehearsal, for example)?
- ☐ Can you combine ambition with being realistic about your prospects?
- ☐ Would you be happy working (and playing) as part of a team or group?
- ☐ Are you willing to gain experience by taking unpaid or low-paid jobs in your area of interest?

... or not?

- ☐ Are you interested in music, but not in a career primarily focused on music?
- ☐ Are your skills and strengths suited to enabling and promoting music-making rather than to direct participation?
- ☐ Do you enjoy organizing, making arrangements and record-keeping?
- ☐ Can you keep calm under pressure and meet deadlines?
- ☐ Are you a good communicator, on the phone and by letter as well as in person?

Think again!

Our first instinct on beginning this book was to put that heading in large letters on page one. For almost any career in music or its support services, as for all jobs in the arts, competition is fierce and there are plenty of well-qualified and talented people looking for work. You will need to demonstrate real interest in and dedication to your chosen career and start as early as possible. Acquiring excellent qualifications, getting yourself known and making useful contacts are all vital, whether your ambition is to be a piano-tuner, an artists' agent, an academic, a DJ or an international opera singer.

Against that it must be said that, if you are determined to succeed, there is a vast range of exciting and challenging musical careers, from soloist to record producer and from instrument-maker to conductor. In this book we have separated the careers into those that use music principally (subdivided into salaried and freelance jobs) and those that support musicians and music-making. Unless you are already absolutely certain which field of music you want to work in, think carefully about your skills, personality, strengths and weaknesses, as well as your academic interests. Ask yourself honestly if you are likely to succeed as a musician or whether you wouldn't be better off working in one of the peripheral areas such as publishing or concert management.

Making music

If you want to make music your career – if, for example, you want to play in a band or an orchestra, conduct, compose or perform as a soloist – you will need to be technically very proficient, competitive, highly disciplined and persistent. In almost all musical careers, excellent qualifications may not turn out to be so important as making the right contacts and being in the right place at the right time, but you are more likely to succeed if you combine both approaches. Acquire the necessary skills and qualifications, but start gaining experience and making contacts as early as you can, by entering competitions, performing in public, organizing concerts of your own music, or taking voluntary or low-paid work in the area that interests you.

Be realistic about your chances of achieving your goal. Unless you are remarkably talented you are more likely to end up in the second violin section of a provincial orchestra, say, than to become the next Midori or Kennedy. Or you may have to spend years working your way up from conducting your school choir to directing a professional group, perhaps by finding work as a conductor's assistant and eventually getting the chance to have a go yourself. Performing, whether as a soloist or as part of an ensemble, will demand hours of rehearsal, and touring will involve tight schedules rather than glamorous sight-seeing around the world. If you are a budding composer, bear in mind that very few make a living purely by composing; you will almost certainly have to take other work to supplement your income.

Many other factors can make a vital difference to your career. Being in the right place at the right time is largely a matter of luck. You can't, for instance, make yourself win a competition that will bring you to the notice of other performers or composers who are already well known and successful, but what you can do is decide to enter in the first place, and decide to keep trying when (as is most likely) you don't win. Enthusiasm and perseverance in themselves will attract the attention of people who can help you advance in your chosen field.

If you're considering self-employment, bear in mind that you will be responsible for keeping accurate and up-to-date records of your income and expenditure, and for filling in tax returns. You will also have to allow some time for generating work for yourself, making yourself known and marketing your particular skills, so you will need to be confident and assertive about your abilities. Your income is likely to be irregular, so you'll have to learn to budget for the lean periods.

Making music possible

There is a wide range of jobs in the support structure of the musical world: music librarianship, promoting concerts, producing and so on. If your interests and abilities lie in this direction, try to work out which area particularly attracts you. Are you an extrovert? Do you enjoy meeting people? In that case you might consider working in arts marketing. Or do you see yourself as a methodical, behind-the-scenes music librarian or administrator?

For all support jobs you must be well organized, multi-skilled and an excellent communicator. Be prepared to start at a fairly low level, maybe in a clerical position, and work your way up. The more adaptable you show yourself to be, the more interesting and varied will be the work you're likely to find.

This book gives you a guide to the range of possible careers in music and the associated areas, with case studies of some of the jobs and advice about qualifications and places to study. At the end of the book you will find useful addresses and publications for further information. The music world is highly competitive, so whichever path you decide to follow, find out as much about it as possible to give yourself a head start.

2 Dots and lines I: salaried musicians

Chorus master

The larger opera companies include a chorus, and many symphony orchestras run an affiliated choir (such as the London Symphony Chorus or the BBC National Chorus of Wales) in order to be able to programme works for chorus and orchestra. Chorus masters are employed to train and rehearse the choir, and conduct it if it gives concerts on its own; there may also be the chance of conducting on some occasions when the choir and orchestra join forces, so this is one path you might follow if conducting is your main aim.

You will need to have a music degree, and preferably a postgraduate diploma from a music college as well. Ideally, you will have trained and had some professional experience as a singer yourself; you'll certainly need a thorough knowledge of the choral and operatic repertoire. You should be able to acquire plenty of experience by rehearsing and conducting choirs at school and college, working with local amateur choirs and attending summer schools or other short courses.

There are very few jobs in this field and it's not something you're likely to go into as soon as you graduate; one route might be to work first of all as a *répétiteur* or accompanist and seize any opportunity to direct choral rehearsals. Any vacancies that are advertised externally will be listed in the quality papers and specialist music journals.

Community musician

In step with an increasing opinion that the arts should be available to all, community and 'outreach' projects have become more and more popular over the last decade and attract funding fairly easily from arts organizations, local businesses and other sources – the Performing Right Society, for instance, sponsors a Composers in Education scheme.

As the name implies, community musicians work in a specific locale and with its inhabitants. Usually they are employed on short-term contracts by councils, arts centres or other interested bodies; sometimes they are self-employed, offering their services on a freelance basis. This job will suit you if you are a performer and/or composer interested in working as part of the community and creating opportunities for local people to participate in music-making. You'll have to deal with people of all ages and abilities, often those who don't normally get a chance to take part in musical activities because they have learning difficulties or are simply unable, for whatever reason, to attend the usual venues. You may be offered a residency in a school, prison, or special needs centre; you may be called on to develop a project of local relevance in collaboration with an artist, dancer, sculptor, film-maker or poet. More information on this kind of work is available from Sound Sense, the national development agency for community music.

Similarly, orchestras, opera companies, festivals and concert venues often employ full-time education officers, whose task is to organize community projects that link with and explain their organization's main work. These posts are advertised in *The Guardian* on Mondays and in magazines such as *Classical Music*.

Military bands

The British military band is generally a large ensemble of wood-wind, brass and percussion, although pipe and drum bands are the norm for Scottish regiments. Even civilian wind bands or 'wind orchestras' generally conform to the military pattern, and many concert works, such as the two Suites for military band by Holst, have been written for the medium. (The brass band is usually amateur and non-military, although many are sponsored by businesses.)

Financial cutbacks in recent years have forced all three armed services to reduce the number of their bands drastically, and each band is now shared by several regiments. Nevertheless, from the age of 16 a young performer still has the opportunity of joining any of the forces and receiving a general music education and a thorough training as a player, with the additional advantages of excellent facilities, professional tuition and a regular salary.

Entry as a musician is usually by interview and audition. The Royal Air Force starts recruits off with a one-year course, including conducting and orchestration in addition to instrumental tuition, after which they are employed in a band. The Royal Marines offer training that comprises performance, conducting, arranging, orchestration and theory of music, leading to an LRSM diploma. The Royal Military School of Music (Kneller Hall) takes recruits for an initial period of military training followed by a one-year foundation course. After that you can pursue studies in performing, conducting or general musicianship, and for over-25s there is the option of a three-year Bandmaster's course. For further information, see Chapter 6.

Military-type bands and brass bands are also run by the police, the fire service and the Royal British Legion.

Music therapist

Music therapy is intended to provide a means of self-expression for people who have difficulty in communicating because of severe physical disabilities or psychological disorders. More than that, it can motivate them to modify undesirable behaviour or to regain memory or physical functions.

Music therapy has been recognized as a career for about 30 years now. With the recent increased emphasis on 'care in the community', there are many opportunities for employment in hospitals, centres for rehabilitation and schools specializing in learning difficulties, where most music therapists will be part of a team that also includes psychologists, doctors, teachers and parents. Therapists may work with various age-groups and problems, from autistic children to elderly people suffering from memory loss. In a typical session, the therapist encourages the client to respond with instrument or voice, so that both of them become involved in singing, playing and listening.

If you are considering a career as a music therapist, you should be a good communicator, musically as well as verbally, and preferably you will have studied music to degree or performing diploma level. Some courses accept graduates in other relevant subjects, such as psychology, but then you will additionally be expected to demonstrate a high level of musical proficiency, including good keyboard skills, even if the keyboard is not your first instrument. Before you apply to train, it would be a great advantage to gain some experience of working with children or adults with learning difficulties, and it would also be a good idea to watch a music therapist in action.

Postgraduate courses leading to a Diploma in Music Therapy are offered by the Guildhall School of Music and Drama, the Roehampton Institute of Higher Education, the Nordoff-Robbins Music Therapy Centre and the Welsh College of Music and Drama. Alternatively you can take a one-year MA at Anglia Polytechnic University, Cambridge, a two-year part-time course at Bristol University or the Introduction to Music Therapy offered by Goldsmith's College.

Orchestral musician

Some budding instrumentalists look on an orchestral career as coming a poor third after solo work and chamber music, but the truth is that there is only a finite amount of work at the top level and as standards rise it's becoming harder to get. If you aim to be a soloist from the start and don't make it, you may be left with no idea what to do next; whereas if you're lucky enough to get an orchestral job you could well find it possible to play chamber music, give solo recitals, teach and so on, in addition. In order to attract and retain players, orchestras are beginning to realize the necessity of offering them more freedom, such as the option of being contracted for just 50 or 60 per cent of their time.

Of course, it's not necessarily easy to get into an orchestra either! Because children are starting to learn much younger, instrumentalists now emerge from college with correspondingly high attainments. On the other hand, not everyone who applies will be temperamentally suited to orchestral life, in which you have to balance retaining your individuality against fitting in with the group, both socially and musically. For that reason if you get beyond the audition you're usually invited to join the orchestra for one or more short trial periods to see whether you fit in. That can be frustrating if you're eager for work, since it stretches the appointment process out to several months.

Orchestral players can be either freelance or on a contract. The BBC orchestras and most provincial ones are contracted, which commits the musicians to a set amount of work but gives them advantages like sickness benefits, instrument insurance and perhaps an instrument loan system. London orchestras tend to be freelance, which lets you pick and choose what you want to do but entails working in different ensembles all the time, with a corresponding lack of input into their running.

Orchestral places are usually advertised in the Saturday *Telegraph* under Musical Appointments, in *Classical Music* and – of course! – by word of mouth. There's also a magazine called *Das Orchester* in which European vacancies appear.

Case Study

David is a sub-principal in the cello section of a major symphony orchestra. He began learning the cello as a child and followed 'the usual route' of County and National Youth Orchestras. He continued to play while reading for a degree in law at university, and subsequently at law school, before deciding he would rather be a professional musician than take up a career in law.

'I'm contracted to do a 40-hour week made up of 25 hours' playing and 15 hours' travel. We know our schedule well in advance, subject to change. For a new programme we usually have two rehearsal days of five hours each – we might have more rehearsals if there are difficult pieces. On the day of a concert we rehearse for up to three hours and the performance usually lasts two to two-and-a-half. Physically it's quite exhausting; but as players under contract we have committees to safeguard our interests and improve conditions if necessary.

'There's more to the job than just playing the notes; the camaraderie is very important. You've got to sit next to and play well with the same person for long periods, which is why we give trials to prospective candidates. Ideally, you look out for one another – if someone's going through a difficult patch personally or having to take time off, you take on their responsibilities, maybe play their solos. And it's the section leader's business to see that all its members feel they're making an artistic contribution and not merely coming into work every day.

'When you're working you have limited time for practice and none for lessons, so it's a great challenge to keep your standard up. In retrospect, one of the most useful things I was taught was how to help myself if I hit a problem in my playing, so I don't need to run to someone else. Another opportunity, which music college provided, was the experience of performing in different types of ensemble: chamber music, opera, large orchestra. I still play in chamber groups, give solo recitals and do other freelance work, besides teaching.

'This is one of the few jobs which you do in front of a very large number of people – not just audiences but 90-odd colleagues who are with you all the time; rehearsing, on tour. That can be stressful if you're the introverted type. But it's marvellous to be playing some of the best music that's ever been written, as one of a team of first-class players with a great conductor. When it all works, it's amazing.'

Organist and choirmaster

These two jobs nearly always go together, because most organists work in a church and are expected to take responsibility for training and conducting its choir. The twentieth century has seen the rise of a new breed of 'concert organists' who are not employed by a church (such as Gillian Weir and, more recently, Wayne Marshall), but they are in effect *solo instrumentalists* (see page 28).

In former times you were expected to study the piano to Grade VI before moving on to the organ, but some teachers now suggest beginning on the organ straight away. Although a qualification is always helpful, you'll find that nowadays it's not essential to be an Associate or Fellow of the Royal College of Organists (ARCO or FRCO). Assuming you've finished your training – and are not immediately aiming for one of the top church or cathedral jobs! – you can contact the churches in your area and ask if there's a vacancy for an organist; or get in touch with your local branch of the Incorporated Association of Organists, which will have information about upcoming appointments; or consult the weekly *Church Times*, which is an Anglican publication but advertises vacancies of all denominations.

The larger establishments, including colleges with a strong choral tradition, often have a place for an Organ Scholar. At universities this usually, although not always, entails reading for a music degree; in any case, it's a way of gaining valuable experience not only of playing for services but of the choir-training the job requires.

The career ladder usually goes from Organ Scholar to Assistant Organist to Organist, then on to a larger church or cathedral with more music staff.

Case Study

Steven is Organist and Master of the Choristers at one of the few British parish churches to have its own choir school.

'I had piano lessons from the age of six, but I was so keen to play the organ that I started learning it two years later, unusually for those days.

'I read for a music degree and was my college's Organ Scholar, responsible for all the chapel music and directing the choir as well as putting on concerts. That gave me lots of practical experience of conducting and organizing, which proved useful later.

'After university I was appointed Assistant Organist to a Roman Catholic cathedral. Because I found myself doing quite a lot of teaching, I decided to get a formal qualification and took a PGCE through the Open University, so that I could fit the course around my working hours. Shortly after that I came here.

'My typical weekday starts at 8.00 am – I don't much enjoy the early starts! I rehearse the whole choir until about 8.45 am, then I give individual singing lessons. In the afternoon I usually go to the church to set out the evening's music. At the end of the school day I walk the boys to church and we rehearse for an hour, then sing Evensong. On Sundays, in addition to Evensong we have the Holy Communion service, preceded by a rehearsal at 9.15 am.

'I have an Assistant Organist, but ideally we'd also have an Organ Scholar who could take some of the work of rehearsing from me. I'm particularly busy at Easter and Christmas and during the preceding weeks. Obviously I can only take holidays when the demands of the job allow; there's no formal agreement, but I get about six weeks off per year.

'I have to maintain a very high standard of music and at the same time keep the clergy, congregation and choirboys' parents happy, so diplomacy is very necessary! A well-sung service has a special atmosphere, and that's the part of my job I find the most satisfying. I also enjoy teaching and communicating music to people.'

Répétiteur

Répétition is French for rehearsal, and a *répétiteur* is literally a 'rehearser'; someone employed by an opera company to coach the singers in their parts individually prior to full rehearsals with the conductor. As part of the company, a *répétiteur* may have the opportunity of taking some full rehearsals and eventually moving on into conducting.

To become a *répétiteur* you will need to be a capable piano accompanist with some knowledge of singing technique. Unless you work for English National Opera, which always performs works in English translation, you'll also be expected to help singers with the meaning and pronunciation of foreign texts, so it will stand you in good stead if you can acquire at least a smattering of the main operatic languages – Italian, French, German and even Russian.

The National Opera Studio at Morley College runs a course for *répétiteurs*.

Teacher

There are few musicians who do not teach at some stage of their lives. Some performers and composers give private tuition in instrumental playing, theory of music or composition in order to supplement their incomes. Many musicians teach full-time in schools and colleges, or give private lessons at home. Others offer extra-curricular workshops to schools and other educational establishments, sometimes as part of an educational unit attached to an orchestra or a music festival, sometimes as freelancers.

Those who teach music are taking on a vital role: by training, encouraging and passing on knowledge they are ensuring the future of music in this country. Whether you teach in a school, in a college or from home, you will be helping to ensure the future of music-making and musical knowledge. Deciding to teach music should not be seen as a safe or easy option; rather it should be seen as a serious commitment to tomorrow's musicians.

Peripatetic instrumental teacher

Peripatetic instrumental teachers are not attached to one partic-ular school or music centre, but travel from one place to another to give lessons. Some parents may be unable to afford the higher cost of private tuition, but the peripatetic service means that their children still get the chance to learn an instrument. You will probably find yourself teaching a range of abilities from beginners to Grade VIII students, entering your pupils for the various per-forming exams set by Trinity College and the Royal College of Music and – depending on the timetable agreed between you and the school – rehearsing children for school concerts or other performances.

Patterns of work vary, but you might find yourself spending a morning at one school, teaching small groups of pupils for half an hour or an hour at a time, and the afternoon at another school. Much depends on the provision of peripatetic services in your county and on the music budget of each particular school. Each county (if funding allows) has a centre for peripatetic teach-ers, which will attempt to find you work once you've registered there. You will need a diploma of some kind, whether in teach-ing or performance. OFSTED has just introduced inspections of peripatetic teaching, so your work will be assessed by indepen-dent observers.

If you're interested in peripatetic work, it's vital to be able to communicate well with children and teenagers, and be confident about working on your own with them. Financially, peripatetic work has complications. A recent change in the law means that peripatetic teachers can no longer be self-employed. If the county service finds you work, it acts as your employer, paying you and deducting tax. If you find your own work at a school, you are that school's employee. You'll have to pay for the music you use for your pupils and any repairs to your instrument. There is little financial incentive to be a peripatetic teacher and no career ladder.

Case Study

*After a degree in Maths and Music, **Lyndsay** acquired an LGSM (Licentiate of the Guildhall School of Music) teaching diploma; she is now a full-time peripatetic clarinet teacher.*

'What I wanted was independence, more than anything. I worked in an office for five years and hated it, whereas I'd enjoyed my previous spells of self-employment. I'd done some instrumental teaching at school and at university, so I contacted the county centre for peripatetics; they recommended getting a teaching diploma, rather than a PGCE. When you're starting out, a qualification helps employers have confidence in you.

'Even when I'd got the diploma, the centre was unable to offer me a job straight away, or guarantee me one or two days' teaching a week, so I did a huge mailshot myself to about 80 schools in the area. Two schools replied and I teach one day a week at each. The other three days' work came through the centre.

'It makes me feel more involved with a school if I can talk to the Head of Music at the start of the day. If there are other peripatetic teachers I might also come into contact with them, but circumstances vary. I plan all my lessons and always bring copies of the children's music, since they're liable to forget it! Some schools have plenty of practice rooms, and their pianos are in tune, but generally I find facilities for instrumental teaching quite poor.

'It's my responsibility to put the pupils in for their Grade exams, although my degree of involvement varies. Some schools, for example, like me to do all the paperwork and play the piano accompaniment for the pupil in the examination. I found it a great help to have worked through the Grade system myself, on clarinet and piano, when I came to deal with it from a teacher's point of view.

'This can be quite a strange job: driving around, sometimes going to two or three schools a day, not always stopping for lunch, sometimes not talking to an adult all day. Often there are waiting lists of pupils and tremendous pressure on you to take on as many as you can, which is tempting because you're paid by the hour. I teach privately as well as in schools; that's fairly typical for a peripatetic teacher. But I'm independent; I'm my own boss; and I love teaching. It's nice not being a "proper" teacher, so that the children see me as a friend.'

Private teaching, see entry under Instrumental teacher (Chapter 3)

School teacher

Recent changes to the school curriculum in Britain mean that the five to 14 age-group need spend only one hour per week on music. With current concerns about the need to raise standards of literacy and numeracy in schools, subjects such as music, art and drama are given less importance on the timetable and less funding. Today's music teacher may find that there is no money for peripatetic teachers to visit the school and little money available for music or instruments, or for taking pupils to concerts. However, most secondary schools have at least one member of staff who is a music specialist and organizes the musical life of the school, in addition to teaching music to GCSE and A-level students. A larger school may have a department of several teachers with enough support from peripatetic staff to enable the pupils to take part in extra-curricular musical activities such as orchestras and choirs, or to put on concerts or musicals. The availability of resources will depend on the school's budget and the importance the Head attaches to the subject.

Class teachers in primary schools teach all subjects in the curriculum, but there is often a music specialist on the staff who either takes all the school's music lessons or gives advice to non-musical colleagues. Extra-curricular music-making such as the choir, recorder group or school orchestra is usually the responsibility of the music teacher; whether there is any support from peripatetic instrumental teachers may depend on the facilities available in the county and the school budget.

There are two common routes into school teaching: either take a degree in your chosen subject and follow it with a post-graduate teaching certificate (PGCE) or take a BEd, for which you study your chosen degree subject over three or four years while learning to teach. The BEd is currently being phased out and replaced by the new degree of BA (Qualified Teacher Status) (see page 68). There are also schemes to attract older people into teaching, most of which involve learning in the classroom alongside an experienced teacher. If you are interested in becoming a school teacher, find out as much as you can about the work and try to get some work experience before you actually embark on your teacher-training course. Most schools welcome some help with hearing children read, playing the piano for choir practice or assembly and so on. It is also a good idea to take a break between your own education and teacher-training. Trainee teachers who have worked outside school or university for a while are likely to have a more mature attitude and more experience of life to offer their pupils.

University or college

If you intend to pursue your musical studies to second degree (MA) or doctorate level, you may then be interested in applying for a university or college teaching post. It will also be helpful to have had some of your writings published, or your compositions performed, depending upon your speciality.

A love of your subject is a prerequisite, as is the ability to communicate it simply and clearly, although you should also be able to convey an idea of its richness and complexity and the fact that all you can do is scratch the surface. All lecturers have to do other duties that are more or less demanding; for example, serving on the Student Liaison Committee or, more importantly, acting as Admissions Tutor or Chairman of the Examiners – two essential, time-consuming jobs which carry great responsibility. Sometimes students study other subjects in addition to music, so you would have to liaise with the departments concerned.

Vacancies are usually advertised in the *Times Higher Education Supplement*. From junior lecturer the normal progression is to senior lecturer; the next step, which comes to only a few, is to a professorship, which tends to bring a lot more administrative responsibility. In many American universities one has to re-apply for one's position every few years until achieving the longed-for 'tenure'; that's seldom the case in Britain at present, so long as you do your job well.

Case Study

Maurice *is a full-time lecturer at a college in the University of London. While still at school he attended Saturday morning classes in piano, oboe and composition at the Royal College of Music, going on to take a BMus degree at Oxford University. For ten years after leaving university he earned his living variously as a music copyist, répétiteur, pianist and composer, before taking his present job.*

'I hadn't really been looking for an academic post, but when a Lectureship in Composition came up I realized that I was probably the right age to try something new. I'm a practical musician rather than an academic – I've always been more interested in writing music than writing *about* it – and they were looking for a composer who could also play and conduct. I heard about it through a personal contact, which is often how the musical world operates. I find "networking" difficult, and wish I'd known at an earlier age how important it would be. It comes more easily to some than others: a famous example is Haydn, who was good at being "diplomatic", whereas Mozart tended to say what he thought!

'My day typically starts with two one-to-one composition tutorials for third-year students. At lunch time there might be a concert given by students or staff, and in the afternoon a second-year composition class, with three or four students. Being able to sight-read at the piano is especially useful: I can play through students' compositions so they can get to hear the music and find out if it's really what they meant. Later I or one of my colleagues or a guest speaker may give a postgraduate seminar on some aspect of 20th-century music. I'm preparing lectures for next year's Introduction to 20th-century Music course and I'll have the resulting essays to mark.

'I set exam papers, decide which scores, books and CDs the library should purchase, and serve on a couple of committees. Also, like every staff member, I'm pastoral tutor to six or seven students who can come to me with any work-related problems.

'Academia might seem a relatively comfortable existence, but it's anything but stress-free if one does one's job conscientiously. You're seldom completely on holiday; you're always at the end of the phone or e-mail, unless you're on sabbatical. But one meets new people; one gets long vacations, and a lot of free time for one's own creative work. I love music and want to share it, especially with younger people. In teaching it's very rewarding to feel you've opened up the students' lives in some small way.'

3

Dots and lines II: self-employed musicians

To succeed as a self-employed musician in any capacity you will need three things:

- talent, without which you shouldn't even be considering this sort of career;
- application, or the ability to keep working even when things are going badly;
- a fair amount of good luck.

More than that, you'll need all three at the same time. As you can see, the only one of the three qualities above that you can control is the second, so be ready to rely on it a lot while you wait for the good luck to arrive!

Many musicians are attracted by the idea of being freelance because it offers them independence and the chance to choose their work to a greater extent than if they were working for an organization. However, be warned that it's a precarious existence; once you abandon the security of a salary, you will have to spend a lot of your time working at finding work for yourself. Make sure you have a good network of contacts before you take the plunge. Freelancing, especially in the early stages, almost always involves irregular employment and thus unpredictable income; to make ends meet you may have to teach or take a job completely unconnected with music.

When you are self-employed you can either handle your financial and tax matters yourself, or employ an accountant, but in either case you need to keep accounts of your business transactions and get into the habit of keeping and filing all your receipts. You'll have to make your own arrangements for a pension, and as a musician you would also be well advised to take out personal insurance in case you're unable to work.

Composer

Concert hall

Generally, composers' income is of three kinds, two of which are royalties. Composers – and authors – can apply to join the Performing Right Society and the Mechanical Copyright Protection Society. The PRS collects and distributes royalties due from performances and broadcasts of their work, whilst the MCPS does the same for commercial recordings (compact discs, etc.). It's the royalties from airplay and CD sales that account for the very high figures that pop songwriters and lyricists can earn and the very great difference that can exist between their incomes and those of the other members of the group. To avoid this disparity, some pop groups make a point of naming all their members as contributors to their songs, so that they will receive equal royalties. On the other hand, it's worth remembering that, according to the PRS, only about five per cent of its members earn more than £10,000 a year in royalties, whereas more than half make less than £250.

The third source of income, for classical and jazz composers, is the commission. This is a fee paid, usually by a performer, for writing a new work. The British Academy of Composers and Songwriters gives guidelines for commission fees, but in practice it's usually not until you're well established that the sum involved represents an adequate payment for your time. Philip Glass, for example, supported himself for many years as a taxi-driver and wasn't finally freed from the necessity of taking non-musical work until the age of 41, when Netherlands Opera gave him his first large commission.

Only a very few composers are able to make a living from composition. The rest, even quite well-known ones, usually have some other source of income, often from a part-time or full-time academic post.

If you hope to become known as a composer, you must persist. Submit your works to competitions and composers' forums; send scores in to the BBC Radio Classical Music department for consideration; offer to write pieces for performers you admire. Try to record your performances whenever possible, so that interested parties can hear examples of your work. If what you're doing has any worth, success will come.

Competitions both at home and abroad are listed in the *British and International Music Yearbook* and in 'Gaudeamus Information', an information sheet issued twice a year by the Gaudeamus Foundation. The latter also contains calls from ensembles and individuals who are looking for new works, which may lead to a performance if not a prize.

Media

Media composers write television and radio theme tunes, incidental music, advertisements, film scores – anything, in fact, that they're asked for – and they pride themselves on being able to work to a very tight brief and produce exactly what's wanted. Media composing is like graphic art, a mixture of creativity and discipline. It's a very hard field to break into; here more than elsewhere, clients want to know what to expect, and so they tend to go to someone they've used before and know they can rely on. Getting started is very much a matter of taking steps to meet producers, directors, commissioning editors and so on, and then selling them your wares. Once you've managed to get a few commissions and an agent or publisher, it becomes progressively easier to get work.

It helps to have some musical training, though not necessarily to degree level. What is really essential is to have your own recording equipment, good samplers, a MIDI set-up, multi-tracking and so on; and if you're going to compete it has to be state-of-the-art stuff. For a media client you need to be able to produce a master quality tape or even a CD. All that hardware represents a high capital outlay, and then of course you have to keep it secure and well insured, which is expensive.

You will be commissioned for a specific project and then probably spend a lot of time with your colleagues, the director or producer; it's important to get to know them and their working methods so you can collaborate efficiently. Unfortunately, media companies are notorious for changing personnel on long projects. It can be confusing to go back after three months and find a different set of faces with a different set of ideas!

Case Study

*Like most composers **Pete** has to supplement his income, and also teaches guitar. When he spoke to us he was working on the incidental music for a television series of wildlife programmes.*

'From an early age film music and so on made quite an impact on me. My first job came about when I was in a recording studio playing with a band, and the same studio was also doing work for commercials and things like that. I played on some of the commercials; then they wanted arrangements and it led from there, little by little. Most people working in the field haven't been formally trained. I was a self-taught musician for years and only later did an external composition diploma at Trinity College, London. If you want to do "straight" orchestral arrangements you need training, but you might prefer to develop a distinctive sound.

'There's a lot of competition for the work, and it's very much a question of being in the right place at the right time, of meeting people socially. I think the first step is always to write a letter, introduce yourself and say that you're interested and then follow that with a phone-call.

'You need a certain skill to discuss music with people who don't speak in musical terms. I don't think I've ever worked with a director, producer or commissioning editor who was musical! That's good in one way, because someone who half-knows about music will start trying to do the job for you. Sometimes, because of lack of communication, people are unrealistic about the time needed and are unsympathetic when you've had to put in hours of work, so you need to be diplomatic and strong-minded.

'My working pattern doesn't fit office hours. I usually work from 10.00 or 10.30 am to 5.00 pm, then break and start again at 8.30 pm. My best working time is late at night. If the deadline is tight I like to clear the schedules so that there aren't other things bothering me. It's wonderful to use your creativity and actually get paid for it, although I wouldn't say that media composition was necessarily the most artistic thing to do. Sometimes you have to work to a very tight brief. It can literally be, "We need fifteen seconds of blue-grass music in this key with these instruments."'

Conductor

To conduct you have simultaneously to take in what you're hearing and transmit something back to the performers through gesture. You can't practice that alone; you have to learn on the job, and unfortunately work is quite scarce. However, vacancies for conductors of amateur productions, choral societies and so on are advertised in the musical press, as are competitions for young conductors. Some music colleges offer postgraduate conducting courses, although you might be better off at a university with a flourishing musical life, where there will be more, and more varied, conducting opportunities. Established conductors also take on pupils, who act as their assistants and eventually get the chance to conduct rehearsals or the less important concerts.

Another way in is to become a chorus master, or *répétiteur* or rehearsal pianist for an opera or ballet company. Ballet companies particularly have work to offer young would-be conductors, because they perform a relatively small repertoire over and over again and will be willing to use you as soon as they feel you're competent. Before then, of course, you'll have played many hours of piano reductions of ballet scores which require you to have eleven fingers on each hand!

A conductor needs a keen ear for mistakes, exceptional keyboard skills and the ability to score-read, although the last isn't so vital as learning and preparing a score for rehearsal. At least 99 per cent of a conductor's work is done before the performance.

*At the age of 30, **Sarita** took stock of her life and decided she would regret it if she never tried conducting. She now conducts her own opera company.*

'I'm a violinist, but I never wanted to play professionally because I'd rather tell people what to do than sit in an orchestra and be told – even though as conductor you miss the camaraderie of being one of the band, and all it takes to make your life difficult is one stroppy player. People think conductors have huge egos, but in fact conducting is about collaborating on other people's musical ideas and making your overall vision palatable to them. In opera, particularly, you have to draw together all these other egos – the singers and orchestra – to operate as a company. It's very difficult.

'There's endless learning of scores to a demanding schedule. I often get up early and go over what I'm going to rehearse that day, so it's fresh in my mind. I'm always looking for and researching new pieces, too. This job involves a lot of travel, which is horrible, so one of the nice things is that I can do my learning at home.

'A lot of conductors get started by forming groups. I set up a chamber orchestra; then I started doing little operas. I used to assist at ENO. People see you working and building up experience and gradually begin to see you as a marketable commodity. I ran an opera company for five years and saw that while there are hundreds of candidates for every conducting job that comes up, there is a national shortage of people who make things happen; so now I'm engaged in setting up another company.

'The academic side of my university course has proved incredibly useful. You know that there aren't any great holes in your knowledge if you can realize a figured bass, compose a string quartet in the style of Dvořák and all that sort of thing.

'If I'd decided to be a conductor when I was 16, I think I'd have had a much clearer agenda, developed my piano playing, done a lot of conducting and as soon as I left university I'd have started ploughing this particular furrow. But then I might not have developed some of the other skills I have.'

Private instrumental teacher

Demand for private instrumental teaching has increased in recent years as local education authorities have reduced or cut peripatetic services to schools. If you are enthusiastic about your instrument and think that you could be patient with learners and communicate well, and if the self-employed life appeals to you, then private teaching will give you the chance of working with people of all ages and abilities.

Almost any musician can offer private tuition, but you are likely to find that an instrumental teaching qualification, such as an ALCM or LRAM, will inspire more confidence in pupils and parents. Private teachers usually give one-to-one tuition on one or more instruments, and not necessarily in the classical tradition only. Some also teach jazz, or flamenco guitar, and some offer lessons in music theory. Many will coach their pupils to recognized standards, such as the Trinity College of Music grade exams.

Whether you teach children or adults, your working pattern will depend on school hours or work commitments, so you will probably find that the bulk of your teaching takes place in the evening or at weekends, and that lessons – and thus your income – will usually stop during school holidays. Initially, at least, you will have to attract pupils by advertising in the local paper, music shops, libraries, colleges and so on, although once you get started word of mouth will help you become better known. (See also *Teaching* in Chapter 2.)

Rock or pop musician

It would be nice to say that all you need for success in popular music is to love playing and have an ear for what sounds good. But it's probably a good idea to have some tuition on your instrument at first, to give you the technique to play what you want. Learning to read music, too, may sound irrelevant but will actually increase the number of jobs open to you.

The small ads in *New Musical Express, Melody Maker, Loot, The Stage* and the like are good places to find 'depping' (deputizing) jobs, and if you regularly put in an advertisement of your own you may also get work that way. If you're trying to join or form a group, you'll find that very often there's a lot of talk and not much action – avoid the sort of advert that says 'Deal imminent'! When you go to an audition you'll know at once whether you can get on with the other musicians. That's one of the most important things – in addition to whether they can really play – and you can spend months looking for the right person or band. In the end the most successful way to find congenial work or like-minded musicians is by word of mouth, and by knowing people who know other people.

The frictions that can develop among a group of musicians who spend a lot of time in each other's company are notorious and don't lead to a good atmosphere for music-making. You can lessen frictions by taking things calmly and being punctual and reliable. Just like any other team, whether musical or not, you all have to be responsible to each other.

Case Study

*Originally trained as a graphic artist, **Charlie** is now drummer for a Rolling Stones tribute band. He also plays in a 'British country-and-western' band, which recently had three of its songs used on the soundtrack of a feature film and is about to make its second album.*

'Although I started hitting home-made drums when I was about ten, I never seriously imagined I would end up drumming for a living – pop music was seen as a very glamorous career and I wasn't very pushy. I played in bands at school and at art school. I'm self-taught apart from a few lessons as a teenager to brush up my technique, theory and sight-reading.

'After art school I played for the Cambridge Footlights Revue for about a year. Previously I'd only played in pub bands; this was professional work, mainly in theatres and with some local radio and television. After that I worked full time as a graphic artist, because I needed the money, and drummed part time with various bands. Some years later my personal circumstances changed and I couldn't do a day job as well as look after my three children. What's good about gigging is that I know exactly where I have to be and when, so I can organize my life.

'I've performed the same numbers hundreds of times, but there's always something to improve upon. I don't enjoy the travelling, or the huge amount of time spent hanging around – waiting for soundchecks, for example. There's hardly any opportunity for sightseeing, so don't expect to join a band and see the world.

'All the band's equipment is stored in a lock-up unit, and insured under a joint policy. Our two roadies transport the kit from there to the gig. I do three gigs a week on average – about 150 a year – from 20 minutes in length up to two hours. Last week we did four gigs in Belgium in four nights, then a fifth on the way back. Musicians who tour with one particular artist have a much more crowded schedule; they might play every night for several months. Our fees go into a common fund and are shared out at the end of each month.

'Conditions on tour vary enormously. Sometimes there are no dressing-rooms and you change in the back of the van; sometimes you're lavishly spoiled.'

Singer

It's best for singers to start training slightly later than instrumentalists, because the voice, particularly the male voice, needs time to develop. Twenty-one is probably a good age to start training in earnest, and your career will start correspondingly later. It depends on your funds, but a good career path for a singer would be to take a university degree first – not necessarily in music, even – and then a postgraduate performing course at a music college. A first degree in modern languages would be a very good choice if you're intending to sing professionally, partly because you may want to look for work in Europe, and partly, of course, because you need a good command of languages in order to sing them properly. Another reason for taking a degree is that it gives you another qualification besides a performing diploma. If you don't make it as a singer for some reason, you'll have another potential career to fall back on.

(Singers are also advised to read the comments under *Solo instrumentalist* on pages 28–30.)

Case Study

Stephen is an opera singer. He studied music at Oxford University and moved on to the Royal Northern College of Music to take a performing diploma. He now sings in opera houses all over Britain and abroad.

'I was always interested in singing and enjoyed it at school, but I wasn't sure that I wanted to make it my career until later. You have to be very realistic if you're going to do this for a living, and keep yourself in good health – stamina is important for a singer. It can be a very peculiar and lonely life, spending weeks or months away from home, living in hotels, working odd hours and having to be careful about what you eat and drink. I've worked a great deal in Germany, because there are more opportunities for opera singers there than in any other country; it has about 70 opera houses as against five in Britain.

'The job gives me enormous satisfaction. I don't think anyone would do it otherwise! There are financial disadvantages, like having to pay vocal coaches or *répétiteurs*, and singers' insurance premiums are huge.

'My schedules vary according to whether it's a rehearsal day or a performance. The day before a rehearsal I check the opera house call-sheet; usually I have to appear at rehearsals twice next day. On a performance day I don't have to spend so much time in the opera house and there's a chance to rest. Unfortunately for singers, most reviewers go to the premiere of an opera rather than waiting a few nights, so they hear us straight after a long period of rehearsal. Not an advantage!'

Solo instrumentalist

Nowhere in the highly-competitive music business is competition so intense as among performers. If you intend to pursue a solo career as a singer or instrumentalist, the first requirement will be to reach the highest possible technical standard. However, that will almost certainly not be enough. You will also have to demonstrate musicality, a gift for interpretation and a sure knowledge of the repertoire. Complete dedication to your craft and a flair for promoting yourself are other vital qualities. Even then, the stark reality is that there are very few places at the top of the ladder for soloists. And, as in so many musical careers, success may depend as much on luck or attracting the right attention as on your gifts or technical mastery.

Instrumentalists should start learning as early as possible, preferably attaining Grade VIII before leaving school. There are two main academic routes to becoming a professional performer: the first is to go to a music college or conservatoire and take a three- or four-year degree course that concentrates on performance; the other is to take a music degree at university (perhaps continuing with singing or instrumental lessons privately), and then a postgraduate diploma course at a music college. Generally, instrumentalists are better advised to go to music college, where you will be more likely to make a wide range of useful contacts and where many of the tutors are themselves past or present performers. Trinity College, London, offers a four-year course in performance leading to a BMus.

If your interests lie in jazz or pop performing, look for the specialist courses offered by some institutions. Leeds College of Music runs a degree course in jazz studies, while the University of Salford offers a BA and postgraduate courses in popular music.

Once you leave college it will be much harder to get experience, so before then seize every opportunity of performing in public. Music colleges and universities hold regular recitals and concerts as showcases for their students' talents; these will provide you with the chance to build up your self-confidence and bring your name to the attention of the audience and of any promoters or agents who may attend.

Another good way of getting yourself seen and heard by influential people – not to mention your future audiences – is to enter competitions. There are dozens of annual competitions in Britain, such as the Leeds International Piano Competition and Cardiff Singer of the World, and many more abroad. Prizes are usually cash and some sort of professional engagement, and even if you are not among the winners, you'll receive some constructive criticism from the judges. The *British and International Music Yearbook* lists competitions world-wide.

There are also many scholarships and bursaries available for young performers (see the *Handbook of Music Awards and Scholarships* for details). A number of organizations give auditions to young singers and instrumentalists, and promote notably gifted artists; among them are Live Music Now!, the Young Concert Artists' Trust, BBC Radio 3 and the Park Lane Group. It's worth getting in touch with them and asking for an audition.

As soon as you have left college and are looking for work, you will need to market yourself well to promoters and agents. They receive hundreds of mailshots, so it really is worth the expense of having an eye-catching brochure professionally prepared, containing a brief biography, photographs, reviews and details of your repertoire. Remember to select appropriate recipients – if you are a budding opera singer, you need only target opera promoters and agents who represent singers. An agent will want to hear you perform, probably more than once, before signing you up.

Solo performing is one of the most demanding careers you can pursue, but the rewards can be enormous if you have the ability, the personality and the determination.

Accompanist

For a pianist, there are many more opportunities to appear in partnership with a singer or instrumentalist than as a solo artist. In such situations 'accompanist' is an inadequate description of your function, and indeed in America the profession is now dignified with the title 'collaborative pianist'. You may become the regular partner of several singers or players and make a very good career that way.

The best way for you to begin is to study piano at a music college that offers accompaniment as a course option (see the *Music Education Yearbook* for details of courses, or get in touch directly with the individual music colleges).

4 Helping hands: music support services

Arts administration

Administration involves a large number of skills and tasks, from secretarial and clerical work to financial management, public relations and concert promotion. All arts organizations, whatever their size, need someone to deal with paperwork, answer the phone and manage the finances. Opportunities in music administration range from working for one person (such as being a composer's assistant) to being part of the administrative staff of a large organization like one of the Arts Councils or a national symphony orchestra.

To be successful at this type of work you should have excellent organizational skills and be familiar with various word-processing, database and spreadsheet computer packages. You will also need to be a good communicator by phone, letter and in person, and be capable of working without supervision if necessary. The day-to-day routine of the job will vary according to your employer; if you work for a large company like the South Bank, you will probably keep fairly regular hours, but if you are the administrator for a small chamber group, you may be expected to work unsociable hours and perhaps tour with the ensemble.

Since there are fewer vacancies in music administration than there are candidates for the posts, it would be to your advantage to gain a postgraduate qualification in arts administration after taking a music degree. Look for a course that encompasses a variety of useful accomplishments such as budget management, marketing, public relations and office skills. When you apply for jobs, bear in mind that they will be scarce, and be prepared to start in a lowly post and work your way upwards. At the bottom of the administration career ladder you are likely to find yourself word-processing, photocopying and filing, but as you move on, more responsibilities should bring more rewarding work. If you start work with a small organization you're more likely to get the chance to try a variety of tasks.

Vacancies are advertised in *The Guardian, The Independent* and specialist music journals like *Arts Business*. It's also worth writing around with your CV – it will go on file and if you seem interesting and well qualified you'll be borne in mind if an opening becomes available. Another way to get your foot in the door is to do some voluntary or low-paid administrative work for local concert venues or festivals (see the section *festivals* on page 34), preferably before you leave university or college. You'll make good contacts and learn at first hand what the job entails.

Artist's agent/manager

Agents deal with the day-to-day marketing, finance and administration necessary to promote their musician clients and keep their work flowing. As an agent, you will be responsible for a number of artists, who might be performers, conductors or composers. You'll negotiate with prospective employers on behalf of your clients, obtaining work, agreeing fees (of which you'll take a percentage for your trouble) and formulating contracts – it will be useful to acquire a working knowledge of contract law. You'll also help an artist's career in its earlier stages, and later, by sending out promotional mailshots containing his or her biography, photos and press reviews.

A successful agent is an excellent communicator with a good understanding of the pressures under which a musician works; indeed, many agents have trained and worked as performers themselves before moving into management. Whilst a music degree is not essential, you'll need a thorough knowledge of the music world, or at least one particular area (say chamber music, or conducting) if you intend to concentrate on that type of client. You will have to build up and maintain a network of contacts with concert venues, orchestras, opera houses, festivals, promoters, publishers and record companies. Some of your time will be spent going to hear or see new young artists; otherwise much of the job will involve phone-calls, bookings and meetings. Your clients may very well work abroad, so knowledge of languages will be a great help to you in international dealings.

If you are interested in a career as an agent, contact the International Artist Managers' Association (see Chapter 7 for the address).

Concert promoter

Promoters take on the responsibility of mounting artistic events, and guarantee the performers' fees, in exchange for the chance to make a profit. If an event doesn't attract the public, the promoter will lose money on it, so a key part of the job is an instinct for what will sell well.

A promoter can be an organization like a music festival, or an individual who either works for a concert venue or runs an independent company. The business of promoting will include booking artists and venues, forecasting box office income, budgeting, organizing publicity, maybe seeking sponsorship, and arranging all the practical necessities such as the performers' accommodation, piano-tuning, sound-checks, programmes and refreshments. The character of the job will vary according to whether you work at a particular venue with staff to help you or run your own business.

Concert promoters need a large range of skills and a vast network of contacts, and must be well organized, calm under pressure and good at getting along with all sorts of people. They also require solid financial resources, so this is probably not a field to go into straight from university or college! But – as with so many careers in music – you can start early by organizing events at school and college. The best experience would be to do some voluntary work for a music festival.

Festivals

Dozens of music festivals take place in Britain every year, some large, some small. There are long-established events with an international reputation, as at Aldeburgh or Cheltenham, and more localized ones like Presteigne or Gregynog. The number of administrative staff necessary for the running of a festival will depend on its size and budget. A large, well-financed organization will probably employ an Artistic Director, who devises the programme; an Organizer, who implements the director's plans; a Publicist or Marketing Officer; a Fund-raiser; box office staff; and various clerical assistants. At a smaller festival one person may take on several of these tasks.

There is also an increasing trend for music festivals' remit to include the development of education and community projects. The ideal is to draw in all ages and social groups by, for example, arranging for composers and performers to run workshops in local schools or other venues. Some festivals employ an Education Officer or team, while others hire professional educators for their outreach work.

The best way to get into festival work is to volunteer as a helper, even while you are still at school if your local festival takes place out of term time. Most large arts festivals that take place during the summer months take on music students to work as helpers in return for food, lodging and a behind-the-scenes view of prestigious musical occasions. In a typical day your duties might include answering phone enquiries from members of the public, ringing around local music shops because a performer has a problem with his or her instrument, ferrying artists to and from concert venues, helping to set out the stage, ushering and selling programmes at a concert, turning a pianist's pages and presenting flowers to a soloist!

If you are interested in this type of work experience, contact your nearest festival or BAFA, the British Arts Festivals Association. Although the work is unpaid, it will give you an excellent opportunity to make contacts, whichever branch of music you are interested in, and to find out your own strengths and weaknesses. Many festival helpers go on to get good jobs in arts administration, but at the very least, if you prove yourself keen and useful, you should be able to ask the senior staff in the organization to be your referees in future applications.

Orchestras and ensembles

The work of an administrator is mainly clerical, so you'll be expected to be computer-literate and to possess the usual office skills: typing, word-processing, photocopying, faxing. Administration for smaller groups can also involve writing out parts and scores, so ideally you'll have studied music at least to A-level.

As administrator you will be the main channel of communication between your group and other performers, venues, the press, the public and so on, so you must be accessible, articulate and friendly, and have a good phone manner. You will certainly need patience and calm, because things can get very hectic at times. Most smaller groups can employ only two or three administrative staff, so you'll also need the ability to work well in a small team and take complete responsibility for your own tasks.

A large organization such as a symphony orchestra will employ a greater number of administrative staff and there may be the possibility of promotion to a position like Orchestra Manager, with a corresponding increase in pay and responsibilities. At the other extreme, freelance ensembles may employ one of their own number as part-time manager and 'fixer', to book performers on an ad hoc basis. If you're already a player and are interested in going into administration, that would be a good place to start.

Case Study

*After taking a degree in music, **Katie** spent several years working for BBC Radio 3 as a production assistant, then became administrator for an early music group.*

'I read music at university because I'd done it at A-level and was interested, although I had no idea what I was going to do afterwards. I knew that

I didn't want to teach and that I probably wasn't going to be a performer. By the time I left the BBC I'd become interested in music administration, particularly with performers in the early music field, and I got this job through having met and worked with the group already at Radio 3.

'Contact with the music and performers is the most satisfying thing: hearing the group rehearse, and going to concerts and recordings. The other side of that is that you can be required to work unsociable hours if the group does – you may be asked to tour with them, or attend recording sessions in the evenings or at weekends. Mostly, though, I work from 9.30 am to 5.30 pm.

'The group records or performs nearly every week, so my normal day involves dealing with the artists, planning schedules, making sure that the music's in the folders, answering the phone, writing letters. Booking venues, travel and accommodation – sometimes a concert-promoter will handle that, but I still have to know every detail because I'm the one everyone's going to ask!

'I work in a small office, very quiet and pleasant, with only one or two other people. That means it's quite isolated except when the performers are around, and there isn't·a lot of back-up, but everyone mucks in. Musicians can be very temperamental people, unwilling to get involved in the practical side but wanting things done a certain way, so you have to watch out for that and be as tactful as possible.

'I'm a violinist myself and I've played in, and been on the committee of, self-managed early music groups, which was useful experience. I also played in school and youth orchestras, which taught me about the practicalities of being on tour from the player's point of view. I know how horrible it is when things go wrong.'

Copyist

The development of music–processing software has been a great labour-saver for everyone involved in writing, performing or publishing music, and it's becoming more and more common for original scores and parts to be produced and printed by computer. Nevertheless, about one-third of professional music copying is still done by hand, so to become a copyist you will need tidy, legible musical handwriting in addition to computer skills. The BBC, which performs a lot of new music, employs copyists; so do orchestras (whose copyist is usually the *Music librarian*) and publishers. Many freelance copyists are composers trying to make ends meet!

There is no formal training for being a copyist and not many job openings, but if you are interested in this work you could try writing to orchestras, publishers and the BBC, enclosing samples of your music handwriting and asking to be considered for any vacancies that arise. There are also commercial music copying businesses that might give you some work experience (these are listed in the *British and International Music Yearbook*). *The Essentials of Music Copying*, by Susan Homewood and Colin Matthews, is a useful reference book.

Instrument-builder

Mass production at the lower end of the market has certainly not put an end to professionals' need for high-quality hand-made instruments, which can command good prices once the maker begins to acquire a reputation. Meanwhile, the growth of interest in early music has also created a modern demand for recorders, crumhorns, rebecs, viols and so on – not to mention keyboard instruments like spinets and regals – alongside the standard orchestral range. If you're fond of a certain type of music, or even a particular instrument, but don't feel you're cut out to be a performer, you may find satisfaction in becoming an instrument-builder. (Another term you may come across is 'luthier', a French word that originally meant 'lute-maker' but is now applied to someone who makes stringed instruments of any sort.)

There are usually no academic requirements for instrument-building courses. Obviously it helps to be able to play the sort of instrument you make; well enough, at least, to assess your own work, although each instrument will eventually be put through a thorough 'road test' by the performer for whom it's intended. Apart from that, you'll need an aptitude for working with your hands and an enjoyment of craftsmanship for its own sake.

Helen *is a builder of violins, violas and cellos.*

'I've always liked making things – even now I'd rather spend my spare time on DIY or gardening than on something passive like reading. I was a cellist at school, but it wasn't until I bought a cello that I realized a profession existed which combined my interests. After an interview and an aptitude test I was accepted by the school of violin-making at Newark.

'Some patience is necessary for the work, but not as much as people think! You need musical ability, not necessarily in performing but in being able to hear the difference in the quality of sounds.

'I find it very satisfying that my work has a physical end-product, an object that I've created. It's nice to go to a concert when one of my instruments is being played. An instrument becomes part of its owner's life, and to that extent so do I: I enjoy getting to know each customer and developing a good relationship.

'The advantages of being self-employed can also be disadvantages. You're independent, but if things go wrong it's all your fault; there's no one to give you support. Your income can be erratic, even when you've built up a reputation, you never stop worrying when business is slack.

'I don't work at home, so a large expense is the rent of a workshop. Another is maintaining my wide selection of mature (at least five years old) wood, which I need in order to choose the right piece for the task in hand. In the early days I also made a big outlay on acquiring tools and equipment; naturally that lessened over the years.

'I spend about nine-tenths of my time in the workshop and the remainder on things like visiting customers, running a stand at trade fairs and travelling abroad to buy wood. I deal with the business paperwork in the evenings.

'It's surprising what's turned out to be useful. My school French and German is a help when dealing with timber merchants, and I'm grateful to my mother for making me learn to type! I wish I'd studied science more – I make my own varnish, so chemistry would have come in handy, and I'd like to know more about the physical laws of acoustics.'

Journalist

Most national and local newspapers carry music reviews, and specialist publications also include longer features, interviews with prominent musicians and news about the music world. Some newspapers and journals employ full-time music staff, but most

music critics and writers either hold full-time employment elsewhere or are freelancers with at least one other source of income
(from broadcasting, teaching and so on).

There is not a great deal of this kind of work available, but if
you are in search of it you must know your subject well and be
able to write about it in a refreshing and interesting way. A good,
clear prose style is essential, as is the ability to meet a deadline.
You'll also need limitless enthusiasm for music, because you'll be
listening to plenty of it – not just the concerts and recordings
you're reviewing, but all the others that provide you with com-
parison and background.

The best academic route for a music journalist is probably a
music degree followed by a course in journalism. However, as
with so many careers, getting started early and building up contacts are also vitally important. Read professional music writers to
see what you think has made them successful; attend music
events; listen to recordings new and old and try your hand at
writing about them. Submit your work to your local papers to
start with. Even if it isn't accepted you might receive some constructive criticism from the editor and make useful contacts. You
could also try sending pieces to relevant publications such as *The
Gramophone, New Musical Express* or *Opera Now.*

Media (broadcast)

Historically, the BBC has always been one of the largest employers in broadcast media. Its current managerial and financial problems are well documented; staffing levels continue to fall, affect-
ed by the running-down of in-house facilities and the quota of
externally-made programmes the corporation is now obliged to
purchase. There are still vacancies, of course, but as Sharron, our
producer interviewee, said, you might do better to set up your
own independent production company than try for a BBC job.

Vacancies at the BBC and in the independent sector are
advertised in *The Guardian* on Mondays. But – as with all arts jobs
– it's much better to hear about them from a contact on the inside,
if you have one. Then it's always a very good idea, and perfectly

acceptable, to arrange to come in and talk to someone who's already doing the job. People are always willing to discuss their work, and it shows that you're keen.

To a certain extent broadcasting depends on 'live' professional music-making, most of which takes place outside normal office hours, so that can mean a lot of evening and weekend work. Similarly, recording studios are sometimes available only at inconvenient times of day. Pay usually includes some compensation for unpredictable hours.

Although it has the higher profile, music on TV employs far fewer people than music on the radio – unsurprisingly, since there are several radio stations entirely devoted to music of one kind or another. For that reason the following examples concentrate mainly on radio; information about work in television as well as radio is given in 'Opportunities for Musicians', a fact sheet published by BBC Corporate Recruitment Services. If you feel that a formal qualification would improve your chances, many universities now offer courses in Media Studies.

Broadcast assistant

With the advent to BBC Radio of what is known as 'multi-skilling', the previously distinct roles of production assistant, studio manager and clerk have been combined under this one title. You could therefore find yourself working, under a producer, on any of the subsidiary tasks involved in making a programme: running the continuity studio and 'playing in' discs for a presenter; editing tape or digital recordings; researching; dealing with the multitudinous paperwork – word-processing letters and scripts, sending out performers' contracts, timing items with a stopwatch, reporting all use of music to the Performing Right Society, and so on.

There are occasional opportunities for moving from Broadcast Assistant up to Producer. Above Senior Producer the jobs are almost entirely to do with administration, particularly financial administration, and no longer involve 'hands-on' programme-making.

Broadcaster

The best advice for anyone who wants to get on the air is to start young if you possibly can. The people with the most impressive careers are those who begin at the age of 14. By 16 they're going out and recording short items and by 20 or 21 they are presenters. So if you're really keen, write in to your local radio station; offer to make the coffee or answer the telephone – local stations are always inviting listeners to phone in, so help is welcome. You won't be paid – even people doing quite responsible jobs in local radio aren't paid – but you'll have an invaluable opportunity to learn by watching what other people do and talking to them about their work. You might acquire other useful experience from voluntary work in hospital radio or travel and traffic broadcasting. Eventually, if your voice fits, you'll be given the opportunity of going on air in a short 'spot'.

Even when you're just introducing music from discs, you need the ability to speak fluently and interestingly at some length without a script, and to sound interested even though you might not be. After all, there are bound to be all sorts of music that don't particularly interest you, but as you still have to talk coherently about them, and maybe carry out interviews, it helps if you can absorb background information quickly and construct a list of sensible questions. For a classical music broadcaster a basic knowledge of how to pronounce different languages is essential, as you may find yourself introducing a German orchestra, under an Italian conductor, playing a piece with a French title by a Russian composer!

Most broadcasters are freelance, which means a certain level of insecurity, but if employers know you can do the job, you'll be offered work. You should beware, however, if popular music is your speciality, as many more people know the subject, and it is extremely competitive.

Case Study

Rob *was a teacher for ten years. For the past 12 years he has worked as a freelance broadcaster for various radio stations and for motoring*

*organizations. He presents a weekly two-hour classical music pro-
gramme on BBC local radio.*

'I got into broadcasting by working for Radio Bristol's Action Line, which
was run entirely by volunteers. That gave me the chance to meet people at radio stations and show them what I could do, because in this
business there's not so much a career ladder as a seizing of opportunities to get your face and voice known.

'Like me, many people in broadcasting have a background in teaching, which gives you fluency and the ability to sound as if you know what
you're talking about, even when you don't! But on a music programme,
if you really didn't know much about the subject you'd soon be caught
out. I've loved classical music since I was 13 or 14, so I've got the necessary depth of knowledge. You can't do this job without being gen-
uinely enthusiastic about music, but there's no point playing only what
you like yourself, because it might not be accessible to the audience.
So you have to be prepared to abandon your particular interests or have
the audience abandon you!

'People need a reason to tune in to a local radio programme when
they can hear the same sort of thing all day on Classic FM. So we try
to be different by offering a taste of the live music that's coming up
locally. In the week before the show I go through all the listings for
details of events during the coming week and try to set up a couple of
guests for live ten-minute interviews. The programme goes out on
Sunday, so my "weekend" is Saturday. On the Sunday morning I select
the music.

'The usual on-air advice is: talk as though to one person. I know a
lot of people listen to the programme – after all, I wouldn't have been
on for eight years unless they did – but sometimes I'm sitting here
thinking, "Who is actually out there listening to this?" And then someone rings in for a competition and my assistant can hear the programme
going on in the background and it suddenly hits us.'

Producer

Every programme is made by a producer, from the simplest – one
speaker introducing music from discs – up to a live broadcast of
an opera or Promenade Concert involving hundreds of people.
(If the live programme goes out on television as well as radio it
will have two producers, one for each medium.)

Many others also contribute to the making of programmes.
The producer's special role – in addition, possibly, to conceiving

the project in the first place – is to oversee everyone else and ensure that the programme is made on schedule. Getting on with and collaborating with other people are thus vital at every stage of the job, except for the solitary activities such as script-writing.

As producer you may be called upon to do almost anything, from liaising with performers and programme-planners, and making sure all the proper bureaucratic procedures are followed, to operating recording equipment and editing the results. There are as many as six separate digital editing systems employed for different purposes in radio, and three or four of those are in everyday use for music, so you'll have to be technically minded to some extent.

Once people are in music production jobs they tend to stay, so it's rare for vacancies to be advertised. When they are, competition is fierce. Qualifications are probably not as important as a strong interest in music, which doesn't necessarily mean specialist knowledge of Monteverdi's madrigals; enthusiasm and the ability to communicate are more important than academic knowledge. Intelligence, common sense and flexibility are vital, though. You need to be able to work on five or ten dissimilar projects at the same time, all at different stages of development, and keep them separate in your mind. And, of course, there are deadlines to meet.

Case Study

*Although **Sharron's** university degree and postgraduate diploma are in Mathematics, she is now a producer in the Classical Music department of BBC Radio.*

'I enjoyed Maths at school, but not the sort I found myself doing when I got to university. As a result I spent more and more time on musical activities that I did enjoy: I ran and conducted an orchestra, played the clarinet in various ensembles, and just listened to a great deal of music. I got to know a lot of the repertoire, which stood me in good stead later. The orchestra in particular taught me how to organize complicated events, raise enthusiasm in a team and lead without seeming to order people around.

'After university I applied for all sorts of jobs and was still undecided about what I really wanted to do when I heard, by word of mouth, that the BBC offered Production Traineeships and that that year, unusually, there was one specifically for music. So I applied and – unbelievably – got it.

'No two days are the same in this job. I like that: I find satisfaction in doing a wide range of things. You have to work odd hours sometimes, but up to a point you can also arrange your time to suit yourself. Depending on the sort of programme you're making, you meet a lot of interesting people.

'If you don't make an effort you can fall into a rut of staying with what you know, but I'm glad to have the opportunity of discovering unfamiliar music. I believe that the arts help to make people's lives more bearable and if, say, I find a piece of music that deserves to be better known and broadcast it, I feel I'm making a small contribution. It's nice getting listeners' letters which tell you so, too. Of course you also receive complaints about your programmes, but that's life.

'Internal bureaucracy has made things very difficult. These days an in-house producer is just one programme-supplier among many, some of them independent, and that gives the Commissioning and Scheduling department enormous power. You have to "sell" your programme ideas much more. When I first started, about half my ideas were accepted; nowadays it's closer to a tenth.'

Music librarian

This term usually applies to the individual who stores and maintains an orchestra's own, sometimes valuable, collection of scores and parts, and sees to the buying or hiring of new material as required. Your responsibilities will usually include making sure there is a complete set of orchestral parts for each piece, inserting bowing and any expression marks desired by the conductor, setting the parts out on the music-desks at the beginning of every rehearsal and collecting them up at the end, and also performing any necessary 'first aid' by repairing parts, making illegible ones legible, copying out new material, and so on. Sometimes an element of arranging may be involved, from the minimal, such as transposing a bass trumpet part for tenor trombone, up to re-scoring a whole passage to cover for the missing tuba. Very often these duties will require you to go on tour with the orchestra.

Music librarians are employed by major orchestras and by any organization that runs an orchestra, such as opera, ballet and broadcasting companies. Publishers usually hire out, rather than sell, the orchestral parts of works they publish and they, too, employ librarians to look after their stock.

For the work described above, you'd ideally have a music degree and some orchestral experience, and to have studied librarianship would be a bonus. There is another type of music librarian who is a member of staff of a university library, or a larger public library, and specializes in music. For that sort of position a librarianship qualification is essential. For further information see *Brio*, the journal of the International Association of Music Libraries; and check *The Guardian* on Mondays for advertised posts.

Piano-tuner

Although the actual tuning is a solitary business, a piano-tuner has to be friendly and enjoy meeting many different types of customer – and each piano has a different character too. Talking about the qualities of sound is difficult enough, and whether you're on the concert platform with a nervous musician or having a cup of tea in somebody's home you must judge what level of technical information to provide. You need practical hands and a keen, although not necessarily musically trained, ear.

In earlier times, would-be piano-tuners would have apprenticed themselves to a piano factory or workshop. That's still a possible route, although these days you're more likely to go to college for a City and Guilds diploma or HND; you can find out about courses and apprenticeships from the Pianoforte Tuners' Association. In the end, qualifications are useful but not as important as whether you can do the job. Usually you're given a 'test tuning' – you tune a piano that has been left alone for six months or so and then someone assesses your work.

There's no real career structure, although concert tuning is considered superior to domestic work and there are a few 'top' jobs, such as working for a famous piano manufacturer, or being the regular tuner for a prestigious venue or an internationally known performer. Most tuners, though, are self-employed, and although that can have drawbacks (for example, it can take a while to become established) it also confers real advantages. Overheads are low, since you work from home: you just need a car, a telephone and advertisements in the *Yellow Pages* and local press. Cash-flow is good, since you normally get paid as soon as you've done the work, whilst you purchase repair materials only as you need them (and probably on account from the supplier).

Case Study

*After school, **Gary** embarked on an engineering apprenticeship, intending to become an electrical engineer. Discovering he was red/green colour-blind made that an impossible ambition, but then by chance he saw a trainee post advertised by the piano manufacturer Kemble-Yamaha.*

'Although I'd played the violin at school, I didn't play the piano at all, but I'd always been very practical, interested in woodwork and repairing things, so I went for the interview. I got the job and for two-and-a-half years I learned about manufacturing and tuning pianos. Then I went to college for three years, in Newark, got my diploma and went to work for an established tuner. I could have become self-employed straight away, but I thought it would be useful to see how a business worked. Also it gave me immediate experience of some very good-quality instruments, at music festivals and so on.

'Then I spent a year in Australia and discovered what a portable trade piano-tuning is: a few tools are all you need to carry. I've been self-employed ever since I came back to England, although it's taken a few years to get established. I have one or two useful contracts; for example with Wells Cathedral School, where I spend 35 to 40 days a year – they have 70 pianos! Otherwise I prefer domestic tunings. I have done concert work in the past, but nowadays I like to keep the evenings free for my family.

'I do five tunings a day, five days a week; that's 25 tunings a week which need booking in advance, so you've got to be organized and good on the phone. I spend an hour every evening in my office in the loft dealing with enquiries and arranging next week's work. That's the part I enjoy least, along with marketing myself. I keep a "rolling" card-file to remind me when customers' pianos are due for a six-monthly or annual tuning; it suits me because I can physically take the card with me and note down any peculiarities of the piano or queries from the customer.

'I still really enjoy tuning pianos. Each one is different and there's an almost creative satisfaction in completing the job well, even if some owners won't be able to hear the finer details of what I've done. On the other hand some will, and they keep my standard up!'

Publishing

Music publishers not only produce and sell printed scores and books on musical subjects, but carry on several subsidiary related activities. The promotion department publicizes the works of contemporary composers published by the house, and tries to get them performed; the hire department (which may employ *music librarians* and *copyists*) rents out orchestral material and parts of works published by the house. In addition, the main stream of a publisher's business involves editorial, design, production, marketing and sales staff. Many people gain experience by working for a music publisher and then set themselves up as self-employed editors, proofreaders, copyists and so on.

Publishing jobs are advertised in *The Guardian* on Mondays and in the music periodicals. As usual it will be to your advantage to take the initiative, write to or ring up publishers and get yourself known, even if there are no vacancies in the area in which you want to work. Having a broad range of interests outside music will work in your favour, as will open-mindedness about genres of music other than mainstream classical – publishers deal with all sorts.

One possible route would be to start off in the hire library, or promotion, in order to get some idea of the work, and then move on into editorial or production. Most of the time, training will be given while you're on the job. If you want to be an editor you will ideally be full of creative ideas, capable of precise, detailed work and good at dealing with people. Obviously not everybody is all those things, and for that reason editors often work in teams.

There is the possibility of promotion, but positions above Senior Editor are managerial or administrative, offering little or no further opportunity to work on specific publications or use your musical skills directly.

Case Study

Ben *took A-levels in Arts subjects, followed by a music degree. Before getting into publishing he worked for a music agent and at the Britten-Pears School at Aldeburgh. He is now an Editor in the Education Department of a London music publisher.*

'I've always liked discovering unusual music and introducing people to pieces they might not know, and I thought publishing would be an opportunity to do the same thing on a much larger scale: after all, to publish something means to make it public. I wrote to lots of music publishers and asked to come in and talk to them, whether they had a vacancy or not, so I could find out about the profession as a whole. One publisher gave me a fairly menial job for a few weeks, which was an opportunity to meet people and talk about what they did. Then I got a new post, which was created in their editorial department. After a couple of years I came to my present job, which was the first advertised position I'd applied for.

'It's important to have an open mind – when I was a student I spent most of my time listening to a huge amount of often rather off-beat music, outside the syllabus. You also need a knowledge of literature and the arts as a whole, in order to be able to put music in a general context.

'Good teamwork is very important. I think publishing is all about getting lots of people's opinions. There's another editor with me in our department, and we work very closely with the production, marketing and sales departments.

'You need to be organized enough to work on several things simultaneously, because it's a combination of overseeing projects that have been accepted and thinking about new publications to suggest to the next acquisitions meeting – we have one every two months. We get a lot of support for new ideas here, and when you've seen a project through the production process and finally hold this pristine new publication in your hand, it's a wonderful feeling! And later on perhaps you hear from somebody who loves the music – in the case of our educational publications, it might even have been the catalyst that got them into music – and that's the most exciting thing.'

Recording company

Comparatively few people work in the recording industry in relation to the size of its market, and of those, only a fraction work in classical music. In addition to the jobs described below, companies employ staff in the areas of administration, management, press and publicity, and promotion.

Information about the professional recording industry can be found in periodicals like *Studio Sound* and *The Mix*.

Producer

A producer working on a studio recording will have much the same function whether the end result is destined for a CD or a radio programme (see 'Producer' under Media (broadcast), page 42). In fact, record companies and broadcasters occasionally collaborate on 'dual-purpose' recordings, which are both broadcast and issued on CD. As a producer, you will work in the control room with the recording engineer: your job is to keep a keen ear on the quality of sound and performance, listen out for errors and encourage the artists to give their best 'performance' – something they may not find easy in the studio.

Recordings of classical music generally aim to reproduce the natural sound of instruments and voices, so edits and overdubs are kept to a minimum. You may decide that certain sections of the music could be improved by re-recording; then part of your job will be to mark up the score with instructions for the editor, indicating clearly which 'take' to use and where to cut from one take to another.

Pop music, on the other hand, is frequently built up layer by layer in the studio, utilizing a lot of electronic instruments or 'sampled' sounds, each on its own 'track'. Even acoustic instruments and voices are often subjected to electronic alteration. For those reasons a producer in the pop world is likely to have the more creative role: you will not only oversee the final balance or 'mix' of the individual tracks, but suggest how and when to utilize the studio's resources (which you will be expected to know all about) and maybe help with the musical arrangements of songs. A pop producer who gains a reputation for contributing to the success of the recordings on which he or she works can command extremely high fees.

Studio (recording) engineer

Under the producer's direction, you have the task of controlling the physical processes of sound recording: operating the mixing desk, deciding on the positioning of microphones, and so on. As in radio, you may be assisted by a tape operator, who performs mechanical tasks (including starting and stopping the tape!) and is probably training to be an engineer.

Retailer (CD sales)

Selling compact discs is a useful first job for someone seeking entry into the music industry; many recording company sales representatives, for example, started out this way. Most shops take on Saturday assistants, so if you're studying music at A-level and want a part-time job, this might be a good place to begin. You'll find you learn a lot simply from hearing a wide range of music played in the shop and from dealing with customers' queries.

But don't think that all the job entails is sitting down all day and listening to discs. It's hard work and the hours are long, beginning before the shop opens with tasks such as starting up the computer, loading the till and opening and sorting the mail. During the day deliveries arrive from record distributors and have to be unpacked, priced and labelled. Reps visit. Mail-order CDs are packaged and sent out. There are new releases to be keyed in, stock-taking to be done and phone-calls to be answered. And all the time, of course, there are the customers!

You must be able to put people at their ease and talk to them about what they want. Some customers know exactly what they're looking for, others want guidance and advice; but most of them aren't very adventurous. They know what they like, so you must cater to their tastes, not force your own on them. Part of the job's satisfaction lies in meeting people and finding out their various enthusiasms. On the other hand, as in any shop work, you occasionally encounter difficult customers.

Vacancies for assistants are usually advertised by word of mouth, so don't be afraid to go into shops and ask. Be prepared to show that you're computer-literate and good at maths, not just because you would regularly have to deal with 11-digit catalogue numbers but because even small shops nowadays use some kind of electronic stock-control system. Employers are likely to be less interested in your musical knowledge than your aptitude for the business side.

5 | Getting started

There are eight steps in scaling the career ladder.

- ◆ **C**onsider what you want to do and how to achieve your goal.
- ◆ **D**iscover as much as you can about your intended career.
- ◆ **E**ducate yourself for your career by choosing the right course and qualifications.
- ◆ **F**ind friends! Start networking, make contacts, try to gain work experience.
- ◆ **G**ive a good impression with a well-designed, up-to-date CV.
- ◆ **A**cquire extra skills – they may give you an edge over rival candidates.
- ◆ **B**e bold – don't be afraid of approaching prospective employers, agents and so on.
- ◆ **C**onsolidate your position by keeping abreast of changes and developments.

Consider

Take a good look at your academic skills and outside interests and decide which aspect of music you find most appealing. Exactly what is it that attracts you? Will it still do so after years of training? Remember that even the most glamorous-sounding jobs involve a lot of hard work and will probably require many years of study. You'll need to think about the cost of your studying: you might have to rely on student grants, perhaps eked out with fairly lowly employment to keep you solvent. Be realistic about the sort of person you are, too. Are you competitive? Can you cope with the pressure of work? Are you good at getting along well with people?

Discover

You'll receive two immediate benefits from being as well informed as possible. First, you'll find it easier to reach decisions about your future and second, interviewers – whether at college or in the employment market – are likely to look favourably on you if you've taken the trouble to investigate the course or post for which you're applying.

Start as soon as possible by getting careers advice from experts. Ask questions and read all the useful material you can find. If you are at school or in higher education, there should be a careers advisory service available to you; if not, your local library will have careers information along with useful addresses for further research. Next, get in touch with relevant people and organizations. Most businesses and educational establishments will be happy to send you information about themselves, and many now have websites. If you can get access to the Internet, browse through the relevant pages.

Educate yourself

You are likely to need some sort of further education or training for almost all the jobs in this book, and you can put yourself on your chosen path ahead of the crowd by deciding on the most appropriate qualifications and courses early on. Look for a course that will give you what you want but also give you useful extracurricular experience. Obviously, what will be useful depends on your career path. If you want to take a music degree and go on to specialize in writing electronic music, find out which colleges and universities offer electronic music as part of their degree courses. If you hope to become a solo performer, it makes sense to choose a course which includes plenty of practical work and opportunities to broaden your repertoire and to perform in public.

The *UCAS Handbook* (see Chapter 8) lists all the courses available in all the universities and colleges in Britain and Northern Ireland and includes contact addresses and numbers. For specialist places of education (such as music academies and conservatoires, or schools of instrument-making), see the *British and International Music Yearbook*. Some useful publications and addresses are listed in Chapters 7 and 8 of this book.

Find friends!

In almost any career, personal contacts can be as important as qualifications. The earlier you start to make yourself known, and the more interest you show, the easier you're likely to find getting on to the first rung of the ladder. According to what career you want to pursue, you can aid yourself by writing to experts in your field (broadcasters, performers, producers), or asking to visit workplaces such as recording studios, or attending professional rehearsals.

Try to get relevant work experience. Volunteer your services in a lowly capacity, if necessary. Once you're in the organization, show yourself enthusiastic, adaptable and willing to work hard. Ask questions and learn all you can, not just about the job that interests you, but how it fits into the activities of the company as a whole. If a vacancy arises, you'll stand a good chance of being considered, and if you want to apply elsewhere you should be able to obtain a reference.

Give a good impression

The first impression a prospective employer has of you will usually come from your CV, so it's essential that it looks businesslike and is kept up to date. Ideally it should be typed or word-processed. If you have good word-processing skills, you can produce it yourself and keep it on a floppy disk for making copies and updating; otherwise it really is worth paying to have it done professionally. Employers in the arts world receive huge numbers of CVs every week, so make sure yours is well designed and accurate. Keep it brief (employers don't have time to plough through pages of detail) and make sure it includes the following:

◆ your full name, address and date of birth;
◆ the names of your schools from the age of 11, with examinations passed and grades;
◆ names of universities or colleges you have attended, and the degrees or diplomas you earned, with grades;
◆ details of any other qualifications or training, for example in word-processing;
◆ list of previous employers and employment, including voluntary or holiday work;
◆ the names and addresses of two referees, one of whom has taught or employed you (ask their permission first);
◆ personal interests, such as hobbies, sports and musical activities outside school or work.

Acquire extra skills

Whatever area of music you're trying to enter, every vacancy is liable to attract plenty of other candidates. Many of them will be just as well qualified as you, but you will still have the advantage if you can offer a little bit extra. For example, almost all administrative jobs now require some word-processing, so it's definitely worth learning to use one or two of the more popular packages. If you're retraining or changing career later in life, take a course in office skills. The musical world is international, so any knowledge of foreign languages will come in handy whether you hope to become a performer (touring abroad), a librarian (ordering scores from publishers overseas), an administrator (making and taking international calls and faxes) or a broadcaster (announcing the names of foreign artists and works).

Other useful skills might range from playing an instrument other than your main study to being able to drive, since many jobs specify possession of a clean driving licence.

Be bold

Even when you know an organization has no vacancies, it's perfectly acceptable to send in a letter 'on spec.' and enclose your CV. From your point of view it can do nothing but good, because most employers keep files of likely candidates who have shown interest in the work, and they may contact you if a vacancy does arise. When you apply, your previous enthusiasm should count in your favour.

If you can direct your letter to a particular person in the company, they will be much more likely to take notice of it. Of course you can always simply put 'Head of Personnel', but you'll probably get a better result if you ring up and ask the name of the person you should address your letter to. Make sure you spell it correctly and use the right job title.

Your letter doesn't have to be typed, but it must be legible and concise. Say why you're interested in working for this particular organization, enclose your CV and a stamped envelope addressed to yourself, and keep a copy of the letter for reference. If you also submit any examples of your work, such as a portfolio, a tape or a sample of your music handwriting, make sure they are copies, as you have no guarantee that they will be returned.

When it comes to filling in an application form for a job or a course, it's a good idea to photocopy the form and fill in a rough draft first. Read the requirements carefully and concentrate on those of your qualifications and skills that are directly relevant to your application. If you are invited to attend an interview or audition, think beforehand about what you can offer and what you hope to gain. Interviewers often ask how you see your career developing, so be prepared to show that you have given that question some thought.

Consolidate

At an interview or audition, an employer will be looking not only for the right qualifications and personal qualities, but also for evidence that you are aware of any new developments or changes in the world of music, particularly those that affect your own work. Keep yourself up to date with whatever is appropriate: new technology, or alterations in arts policy or the music education curriculum. If you are already in a job, ask to take training courses in relevant subjects. If you have a variety of marketable skills, you should always be able to find work.

6 Where to study

Choosing the right course: the first step to success

Whatever type of qualification you intend to take, find out as much as possible about the courses on offer before you apply. Courses vary a great deal, so read the prospectuses carefully and write to, phone or e-mail the registrar or course administrator for further information. When you are interviewed for a place, try to talk to some current students there as well as asking questions during your interview. Make sure that this is the right course for you. Mention any particular interests you have, such as early music or gamelan, and find out whether you will be able to pursue them during your time there.

One way to help you decide what you really want to study is to take a summer course, a part-time course or an evening class in your chosen subject before you start to apply for a college or university place. Your local library will have a list of evening classes on offer; summer schools and short courses are listed in the *British and International Music Yearbook*.

Below we have listed places to study grouped under careers. There isn't room to include every institution offering every aspect of music, so we have tried to give you the most likely places to study. Full details of all music courses can be found in the *Music Education Yearbook*. There are also useful contact addresses in Chapter 7.

Music degrees

Undergraduate and postgraduate degrees in music are available at the majority of universities in Britain and Northern Ireland and at a few colleges of higher education. Music colleges and conservatoires offer specialist courses such as performing diplomas and postgraduate qualifications as well as general music degrees.

Courses differ greatly in range and style: some are very academic, others offer options or modules in computer-based music, ethnomusicology or composing for film and theatre. In some music departments, performance, composition, orchestration and conducting are compulsory for all students; elsewhere they are optional. When you are applying, look for the facilities and opportunities that would be most relevant to you in reaching your career goal. For example, is there an organ? Does the department have an orchestra, choir or early music group? Does the course include jazz or electronic music?

For details of all music courses around the country, consult the *Music Education Yearbook*, the *UCAS Handbook* or the *CRAC Handbook*. To find out more about National Vocational Qualifications (NVQs) in the arts, contact METIER, the organization which set up the Modern Apprenticeship Framework. If you need information about scholarships and special grants, consult the *Handbook of Music Awards and Scholarships*, the *Directory of Grant-Making Trusts*, the *Grants Register* or *Awards for Postgraduate Study at Commonwealth Universities* (details are given in Chapter 8).

Specialized courses

Accompanying

There are postgraduate courses in piano accompaniment at most of the conservatoires. See the *Music Education Handbook* for further information, or contact the individual institutions. An MA degree in Piano Accompaniment is offered by **Christ Church College Canterbury**, North Holmes Road, Canterbury, Kent CT1 1QU; Tel: 01227 767700.

Arts administration

Anglia Polytechnic University, East Road, Cambridge CB1 1PT; Tel: 01223 363271; Fax: 01223 352900

City University, Department of Arts Policy and Management, Frobisher Crescent, Barbican, London EC2Y 8HB; Tel: 0171 477 8000; Fax: 0171 477 8887
e-mail: artspol@city.ac.uk

Dartington College of Arts, Music Department, Totnes, Devon TQ9 6EJ; Tel: 01803 862224; Fax: 01803 863569

De Montfort University, Performing Arts Department, Scraptoft Campus, Leicester LE7 9SU; Tel: 0116 255 1551; Fax: 0116 250 6199

Durham University, Business School, Mill Hill Lane, Durham DH1 3LB; Tel: 0191 374 2233; Fax: 0191 374 1230
e-mail: mba.ft@durham.ac.uk

University of Northumbria, Department of Historical and Critical Studies, Squires Building, Newcastle upon Tyne NE1 8ST; Tel: 0191 227 4933

Roehampton Institute, Roehampton Lane, London SW15 5PH; Tel: 0181 392 3269; Fax: 0181 392 3289
e-mail:hamdanic@roehampton.ac.uk

Warwick University, Centre for the Study of Cultural Policy, Coventry CV4 7AL; Tel: 01203 523020; Fax: 01203 524446

Band musician

Barnsley College, Church Street, Barnsley, South Yorkshire S75 1BP; Tel: 01226 730 191
e-mail: music@barnsley.ac.uk

University of Salford, Department of Music, Adelphi, Peru Street, Salford M3 6EQ; Tel: 0161 295 5000; Fax: 0161 295 6106

Choral singing

Scholarships are available at many universities, including Bangor, Bristol, Cambridge, Cardiff, East Anglia, Glasgow, Hull, Leeds, Oxford, Surrey, Sussex and York; and at colleges such as the Royal Holloway and Bedford New College and the Welsh College of Music and Drama. Full details can be found in the *Music Education Yearbook*. For external scholarships and awards, see the *Handbook of Music Awards and Scholarships*.

Community musician

Community Music Ltd, 35 Union Street, London SE1 1SD; Tel: 0171 234 0900; Fax: 0171 403 2611
e-mail: postmaster@communitymusic.org

York University, York YO1 5DD; Tel: 01904 432446; Fax: 01904 432450
e-mail: music@york.ac.uk

Composition

Most undergraduate music degree courses include an element of original composition, but for a specific qualification in composition, refer to the *Music Education Yearbook* for details of the many different postgraduate diplomas and degrees available at music colleges and universities. Courses offered range from composing for film and television to composing for schools.

Conducting

Some universities and music colleges offer conducting as an option as part of the undergraduate degree, and some music colleges and conservatoires offer postgraduate conducting courses or scholarships, so check the *Music Education Yearbook* for details of each course or write to individual institutions for prospectuses.

Electronic music

University of Hertfordshire, School of Information Sciences, College Lane, Hatfield, Herts AL10 9AB;Tel: 01707 284330; Fax: 01707 285098

Kingston University, School of Music, Kingston Hill Centre, Kingston-on-Thames, Surrey KT2 7LB;Tel: 0181 547 7149; Fax: 0181 547 7118

University of Leeds, Department of Music, Leeds LS2 9JT;Tel: 0113 233 2583; Fax: 0113 233 2586

York University,York YO1 5DD;Tel: 01904 432446; Fax: 01904 432450
e-mail: music@york.ac.uk

Ethnomusicology

King Alfred's College, Sparkford Road, Winchester, Hants SO22 4NR;Tel: 01962 841515; Fax: 01962 842280

Kingston University, School of Music, Kingston Hill Centre, Kingston-on-Thames, Surrey KT2 7LB;Tel: 0181 547 7149; Fax: 0181 547 7118

Instrument-building and repairing

Leeds College of Music, 3 Quarry Hill, Leeds LS2 7PD;Tel: 0113 222 3400; Fax: 0113 243 8798

London Guildhall University, Sir John Cass Department of Design and Technology, 41 Commercial Road, London E1 1LA; Tel: 0171 320 1842; Fax: 0171 320 1830

Merton College, London Road, Morden, Surrey SM4 5QX; Tel: 0181 640 3001; Fax: 0181 640 0835

Newark and Sherwood College, School of Violin, Woodwind and Piano Technology, Friary Road, Newark, Nottinghamshire NG24 1PB; Tel: 01636 680680; Fax: 01636 680681
e-mail: mhunt@newark.ac.uk

Royal National College for the Blind, Piano Tuning and Repairs, College Road, Hereford HR1 1EB; Tel: 01432 265725; Fax: 01432 353478

Stevenson College, Carrickvale Centre, Stenhouse Street West, Edinburgh EH11 3EP; Tel: 0131 535 4621; Fax: 0131 535 4622

Jazz

Leeds College of Music, 3 Quarry Hill, Leeds LS2 7PD; Tel: 0113 222 3400; Fax: 0113 243 8798

Military bands

Royal Marines School of Music, HMS Nelson, Queen Street, Portsmouth PO1 3HH; Tel: 01705 722351

Royal Military School of Music, Kneller Hall, Twickenham, Middlesex TW2 7DU; Tel: 0181 898 5533, ext. 8623; Fax: 0181 898 7906

Royal Air Force Headquarters Music Services, RAF Uxbridge, Middlesex UB10 0RZ; Tel: 01895 237 144, ext. 6345; Fax: 01895 810 846

Music therapy

Anglia Polytechnic University, Music and Performing Art Division, East Road, Cambridge CB1 1PT; Tel: 01223 363271; Fax: 01223 352935

Bristol University, Music Department, Victoria Rooms, Queens Road, Clifton, Bristol BS8 1SA; Tel: 0117 954 5032; Fax: 0117 954 5033
e-mail: john.pickard@bristol.ac.uk

Goldsmiths College, University of London, Department of Professional and Community Education, Lewisham Way, London SE14 6NW; Tel: 0171 919 7229

Guildhall School of Music and Drama, Silk Street, Barbican, London EC2Y 8DT; Tel: 0171 628 2571; Fax: 0171 256 9438

Nordoff-Robbins Music Therapy Centre, 2 Lissenden Gardens, London NW5 1PP; Tel: 0171 267 4496; Fax: 0171 267 4369

Roehampton Institute, Music Department, Southlands College, 80 Roehampton Lane, London SW15 5SL; Tel: 0181 392 3432; Fax: 0181 392 3435
e-mail: music@roehampton.ac.uk

Welsh College of Music and Drama, Castle Grounds, Cathays Park, Cardiff CF1 3ER; Tel: 01222 342854; Fax: 01222 344906
e-mail: music.admissions@wcmd.ac.uk

Organ

Organ scholarships are available at a number of universities, including Bangor, Birmingham, Bristol, Cambridge, Cardiff, East Anglia, Edinburgh, Glasgow, Huddersfield, Hull, Leeds, Oxford, Sheffield, Surrey, Sussex and Warwick; and at colleges such as the Roehampton Institute, Royal Holloway and Bedford New College and the Welsh College of Music and Drama.

External scholarships and awards, to enable the recipient to study with the teacher of their choice, are also available (see the *Handbook of Music Awards and Scholarships*).

Performing

Birmingham Conservatoire, University of Central England, Paradise Place, Birmingham B3 3HG; Tel: 0121 331 5901; Fax: 0121 331 5906
e-mail: conservatoire@uce.ac.uk

Guildhall School of Music and Drama, Silk Street, Barbican, London EC2Y 8DT; Tel: 0171 628 2571; Fax: 0171 256 9438

Leeds College of Music, 3 Quarry Hill, Leeds LS2 7PD; Tel: 0113 222 3400; Fax: 0113 243 8798

London College of Music and Media at Thames Valley University, St Mary's Road, Ealing, London W5 5RF; Tel: 0181 231 2304; Fax: 0181 231 2546

National Opera Studio, Morley College, 61 Westminster Bridge Road, London SE1 7HT; Tel: 0171 928 6833; Fax: 0171 928 1810

Royal Academy of Music, Marylebone Road, London NW1 5HT; Tel: 0171 873 7373; Fax: 0171 873 7374

Royal College of Music, Prince Consort Road, London SW7 2BS; Tel: 0171 589 3643; Fax: 0171 589 7740

Royal Northern College of Music, 124 Oxford Road, Manchester M13 9RD; Tel: 0161 907 5200; Fax: 0161 273 7611

Royal Scottish Academy of Music and Drama, 100 Renfrew Street, Glasgow G2 3DB; Tel: 0141 332 4101; Fax: 0141 332 8901
e-mail: registry@rsamd.ac.uk

Trinity College of Music, 11–13 Mandeville Place, London W1M 6AQ; Tel: 0171 935 5773; Fax: 0171 224 6278
e-mail: info@tcm.ac.uk

Welsh College of Music and Drama, Castle Grounds, Cathays Park, Cardiff CF1 3ER; Tel: 01222 342854; Fax: 01222 344906
e-mail: music.admissions@wcmd.ac.uk

Popular music

Barnsley College, Church Street, Barnsley, South Yorkshire S75 1BP; Tel: 01226 730191
e-mail: music@barnsley.ac.uk

Leeds College of Music, 3 Quarry Hill, Leeds LS2 7PD; Tel: 0113 222 3400; Fax: 0113 243 8798

London College of Music and Media at Thames Valley University, St Mary's Road, Ealing, London W5 5RF; Tel: 0181 231 2304; Fax: 0181 231 2546

Newcastle College, Faculty of Visual and Performing Arts, Maple Terrace, Newcastle upon Tyne NE4 7SA; Tel: 0191 200 4000; Fax: 0191 272 4020

University of Salford, Department of Music, Adelphi, Peru Street, Salford M3 6EQ; Tel: 0161 295 5000; Fax: 0161 295 6106

Répétiteur

National Opera Studio, Morley College, 61 Westminster Bridge Road, London SE1 7HT; Tel: 0171 928 6833; Fax: 0171 928 1810

Sound engineering/recording technology

ALCHEMEA, College of Audio Engineering, Windsor Street, London N1 8QH; Tel: 0171 359 4035; Fax: 0171 359 4027
e-mail: info@alchemea.demon.co.uk

Bangor University of Wales, Department of Music, College Road, Bangor, Gwynedd LL57 2DG; Tel: 01248 382181; Fax: 01248 370297
e-mail: mus018@bangor.ac.uk

Bournemouth University, Department of Media Arts and Communication, Poole House, Talbot Campus, Fern Barrow, Poole, Dorset BH12 5BB; Tel: 01202 524111

City College Manchester, Arden Centre, Sale Road, Northenden, Manchester M23 0DD; Tel: 0161 957 1721

City University, Northampton Square, London EC1V 0BH; Tel: 0171 477 8284; Fax: 0171 477 8576

Derby University, Western Road, Mickleover, Derby DE3 5GX; Tel: 01332 622222; Fax: 01332 514323

Edinburgh University, Faculty of Music, Alison House, Nicholson Square, Edinburgh EH8 9DF; Tel: 0131 650 2423; Fax: 0131 650 2425

Gateway School of Recording, Music Technology and Music Business Studies, Kingston Hill Centre, Kingston-upon-Thames, Surrey KT2 7LB; Tel: 0181 549 0014; Fax: 0181 547 7337

Glasgow University, Department of Music, 14 University Gardens, Glasgow G12 8QH; Tel: 0141 330 4093; Fax: 0141 330 3518

Keele University, Department of Music, Keele, Staffordshire ST5 5BG; Tel and Fax: 01782 583 295
e-mail: mua09@mus.keele.ac.uk

London College of Music and Media at Thames Valley University, St Mary's Road, Ealing, London W5 5RF; Tel: 0181 231 2304; Fax: 0181 231 2546

Media Production Facilities, Bon Marché Building, Ferndale Road, London SW9 8EJ; Tel: 0171 737 7152; Fax: 0171 738 5428

Newcastle College, Faculty of Visual and Performing Arts, Rye Hill Campus, Scotswood Road, Newcastle upon Tyne NE4 7SA; Tel: 0191 200 4211; Fax: 0191 200 4729
e-mail: enquiries@ncl-coll.ac.uk

Perth College, Faculty of Arts, School of Music and Audio Engineering, Crieff Road, Perth PH1 2NX; Tel: 01738 621171; Fax: 01738 440050

Rose Bruford College, School of Production, Lamorbey Park, Sidcup, Kent DA15 9DF; Tel: 0181 300 3024; Fax: 0181 308 0542 e-mail: admiss@bruford.ac.uk

Surrey University, Department of Music, School of Performing Arts, Guildford, Surrey GU2 5XH; Tel: 01483 259317; Fax: 01483 259386 e-mail music@surrey.ac.uk

University of North London, School of Communications Technology and Mathematical Sciences, 166–220 Holloway Road, London N7 8BD; Tel: 0171 607 2789; Fax: 0171 753 7002

University of Salford, Department of Music, Adelphi, Peru Street, Salford M3 6EQ; Tel: 0161 295 5000; Fax: 0161 295 6106

Teaching

Classroom

One-year Postgraduate Certificate in Education (PGCE) and three- or four-year Bachelor of Education (BEd) courses are available at many colleges and universities. The BEd course is in the process of being replaced by a BA(QTS) (Qualified Teacher Status). The *UCAS Handbook* gives details of where to study, while information about individual courses is available in the *Music Education Yearbook*.

Instrumental

British Suzuki Institute, 39 High Street, Wheathampstead, Herts AL4 8BB; Tel: 01582 832424; Fax: 01582 834488

International Centre for Research in Music Education, University of Reading, Bulmershe Court, Reading RG6 1HY; Tel: 0118 931 8843, ext. 482

7 Useful addresses

Arts Council of England, 14 Great Peter Street, London SW1P 3NQ; Tel: 0171333 0100; Fax: 0171 973 6590

Arts Council of Northern Ireland, MacNiece House, 75–77 Malone Road, Belfast; Tel: 01232 385200; Fax: 01232 661715

Arts Council of Wales, 9 Museum Place, Cardiff CF1 3NX; Tel: 01222 376500; Fax: 01222 221447

Associated Board of the Royal Schools of Music, 14 Bedford Square, London WC1B 3JG; Tel: 0171 636 5400; Fax: 0171 436 4520
e-mail: chiefexec@abrsm.ac.uk

Association of British Choral Directors (ABCD), 46 Albert Street, Tring, Herts HP23 6AU; Tel and Fax: 01442 891633
e-mail: marie.louise.petit@abcd.org.uk

Association of British Orchestras, Francis House, Francis Street, London SW1P 1DE; Tel: 0171 828 6913; Fax: 0171 931 9959
e-mail: abo@orchestranet.co.uk

Association of Professional Music Therapists, 38 Pierce Lane, Fulbourn, Cambridge CB1 5DL; Tel: 01223 880377; Fax: 01223 881 679
e-mail: apmtcamb@aol.com

BBC Corporate Recruitment Services, PO Box 7000, London W5 2WY; Tel: 0181 749 7000; Fax: 0181 231 9234

BBC Radio Classical Music Dept, Broadcasting House, London W1A 1AA; Tel: 0171 580 4468 (Contemporary music: Andrew Kurowski, Editor, Specialist Programmes)

British Academy of Composers and Songwriters, The Penthouse, 4 Brook Street, London W1Y 1AA; Tel: 0171 629 0992 or 629 4828; Fax: 0171 629 0993

British Arts Festivals Association, 3rd Floor, The Library, 77 Whitechapel High Street, London E1 7QX; Tel: 0171 247 4667; Fax: 0171 247 5010
e-mail: bafa@netcomuk.co.uk

British Federation of Brass Bands, 17 Kiln Way, Badgers Dene, Grays, Essex RM17 5JE; Tel: 01375 375831; Fax: 01375 391246
e-mail: bfbb@clara.net

British Federation of Festivals, Festivals House, 198 Park Lane, Macclesfield, Cheshire SK11 6UD; Tel: 01625 428297; Fax: 01625 503229
e-mail: festivals@compuserve.com

British Music Information Centre, 10 Stratford Place, London W1N 9AE; Tel: 0171 499 8567; Fax: 0171 499 4795
e-mail: bmic@bmic.co.uk

Careers and Occupational Information Centre, PO Box 348, Bristol BS99 7FE

Careers Research and Advisory Centre (CRAC), Sheraton House, Castle Park, Cambridge CB3 0AX; Tel: 01223 460277; Fax: 01223 311708
e-mail: enquiries@crac.org.uk

Channel 4 Television Corporation, 124 Horseferry Road, London SW1P 2TX; Tel: 0171 396 4444; Fax: 0171 306 8366

Community Music Ltd, 35 Union Street, London SE1 1SD; Tel: 0171 234 0900; Fax: 0171 403 2611
e-mail: postmaster@communitymusic.org

Community Music Wales, 2 Leckwith Place, Canton, Cardiff CF1 8PA; Tel and Fax: 01222 387620
e-mail: cmw@mrcl.poptel.org.uk

Department for Education and Employment, Sanctuary Buildings, Great Smith Street, London SW1 3BT; Tel: 0171 925 5000; Fax: 0171 925 6000

Department of Education for Northern Ireland, Rathgael House, Balloo Road, Bangor, County Down BT19 7PR; Tel: 01247 279000; Fax: 01247 279100

Early Music Network, 31 Abdale Road, London W12 7ER; Tel: 0181 743 0302; Fax: 0181 743 0996
e-mail: glyn@earlymusicnet.demon.co.uk

Gaudeamus Foundation, Swammerdamstraat 38, 1091 RV Amsterdam, The Netherlands; Tel: +31-20-694 7349; Fax: +31-20-694 7258
e-mail: gaud@xs4all.nl

Incorporated Association of Organists, 11 Stonehill Drive, Bromyard, Herefordshire HR7 4XB; Tel: 01885 483155; Fax: 01885 488609

Incorporated Society of Musicians (ISM), 10 Stratford Place, London W1N 9AE; Tel: 0171 629 4413; Fax: 0171 408 1538
e-mail: membership@ism.org

Institute of Musical Instrument Technology, 8 Chester Court, Albany Street, London NW1 4BU (written enquiries only)

International Artist Managers' Association (IAMA), 41a Lonsdale Road, London W11 2BY; Tel: 0171 243 2598; Fax: 0171 792 2655
e-mail: iama@easynet.co.uk

International Association of Music Libraries, County Library Headquarters, Walton Street, Aylesbury, Bucks HP20 1UU; Tel: 01296 382 266; Fax: 01296 382274
e-mail: mroll@buckscc.gov.uk

International Society for Music Education (ISME), University of Reading, Bulmershe Court, Reading RG6 1HY; Tel and Fax: 0118 931 8846
e-mail: e.smith@reading.ac.uk

Jazz Services Ltd, Room 518, 5th Floor, Africa House, 64 Kingsway, London WC2B 6BD, Tel: 0171 405 0737 or 0747; Fax: 0171 405 0828
e-mail: jazz@dial.pipex.com

Live Music Now!, 4 Lower Belgrave Street, London SW1W 0LJ; Tel: 0171 730 2205; Fax: 0171 730 3641
e-mail: lmnlondon@compuserve.com

METIER, Glyde House, Glydegate, Bradford BD5 0BQ; Tel: 01274 738800; Fax: 01274 391566
e-mail: admin@metier.org.uk

Music and the Deaf, Kirklees Media Centre, 7 Northumberland Street, Huddersfield HD1 1RL; Tel: 01484 425 551; Fax: 01484 425560
e-mail: matd@architechs.com

Music Education Council, 54 Elm Road, Hale, Altrincham, Cheshire WA15 9QP; Tel: 0161 928 3085; Fax: 0161 929 9648
e-mail: ahassan@easynet.co.uk

Music for Youth, 102 Point Pleasant, London SW18 1PP; Tel: 0181 870 9624; Fax: 0181 870 9935
e-mail: mfy@globalnet.co.uk

Music Publishers Association Ltd, 3rd Floor, Strandgate, 18–20 York Buildings, London WC2N 6JU; Tel: 0171 839 7779; Fax: 0171 839 7776
e-mail: mpa@musicpublishers.co.uk

National Music and Disability Information Service, Riverside House, Rattlesden, Bury St Edmunds, Suffolk IP30 0SF; Tel: 01449 736287; Fax: 01449 737649
e-mail: 100256.30@compuserve.com

Park Lane Group, c/o John Woolf; Tel: 0171 255 1025

Pianoforte Tuners' Association, 10 Reculver Road, Herne Bay, Kent CT6 6LD; Tel and Fax: 01227 368808

Performing Right Society (PRS), Copyright House, 29–33 Berners Street, London W1P 4AA; Tel: 0171 580 5544; Fax: 0171 306 4455
e-mail: info@prs.co.uk

The Radio Authority, Holbrook House, 14 Great Queen Street, Holborn, London WC2B 5DG; Tel: 0171 430 2724; Fax: 0171 405 7062

Royal College of Organists, 7 St Andrew Street, Holborn, London EC4A 3LQ; Tel: 0171 936 3606; Fax: 0171 353 8244

Royal National Institute for the Blind (RNIB), Music Education Advisory Service, National Education Services, Garrow House, 190 Kensal Road, London W10 5BT; Tel: 0181 968 8600; Fax: 0181 960 3593
e-mail: szimmermann@rnib.org.uk

Royal School of Church Music, Cleveland Lodge, Westhumble Street, Westhumble, Dorking, Surrey RH5 6BW; Tel: 01306 877676; Fax: 01306 877260

Scottish Arts Council, 12 Manor Place, Edinburgh EH3 7DD; Tel: 0131 226 6051; Fax: 0131 225 9833
e–mail: administrator.sac@artsfb.org.uk

Scottish Community Education Council, Rosebery House, 9 Haymarket Terrace, Edinburgh EH12 5EZ; Tel: 0131 313 2488; Fax: 0131 313 6800
e–mail: scec@scec.dircon.co.uk

Scottish Office Education Department, Victoria Quay, Edinburgh EH6 6QQ; Tel: 0131 556 8400

Society for the Promotion of New Music (SPNM), Francis House, Francis Street, London SW1P 1DE; Tel: 0171 828 9696; Fax: 0171 931 9928
e–mail: spnm@spnm.org.uk

Sonic Arts Network, London House, 271–73 King Street, London W6 9LZ; Tel: 0181 741 7422; Fax: 0181 741 7433
e–mail: rachel@sonicart.demon.co.uk

Sound Sense (National Community Music Association), Riverside House, Rattlesden, Bury St Edmunds IP30 0SF; Tel: 01449 736287; Fax: 01449 737649
e–mail: 100256.30@compuserve.com

UCAS (Universities and Colleges Admissions Service), Fulton House, Jessop Avenue, Cheltenham Glos. GL50 3SH; Tel: 01242 227788; Fax: 01242 221622
e–mail: enq@ucas.ac.uk

Welsh Education Office, Crown Buildings, Cathays Park, Cardiff CF1 3NQ; Tel: 01222 825831

Welsh Music Information Centre, ASS Library, University of Wales, Corbett Road, Cardiff CF1 1XL (written enquiries only)

Young Concert Artists' Trust, 23 Garrick Street, London WC2E 9AX; Tel: 0171 379 8477; Fax: 0171 379 8467

8 Useful publications

The lending, reference or music departments of your local library will probably stock many of these publications already; if not, they will order specific titles for you on request.

Books

Awards for Postgraduate Study at Commonwealth Universities 1997-99, Association of Commonwealth Universities, London.

Barbour, S (ed) *British Performing Arts Yearbook*, published annually, Rhinegold, London

British Qualifications, published annually, Kogan Page, London

Burston, D (ed) (1997) *An A–Z of Careers and Jobs*, Kogan Page, London

The CRAC Handbook, published annually, Careers Research and Advisory Centre, Cambridge

Directory of Grant-Making Trusts (1997) 15th edn, Charities Aid Foundation, West Malling, Kent

Dollin, L (ed) *Music Education Yearbook*, published annually, Rhinegold, London

Ford, T (ed) *The Musician's Handbook*, Rhinegold, London

The Grants Register, Macmillan, London

Handbook of Music Awards and Scholarships, published annually, Musicians' Benevolent Fund, London

Homewood, S and Matthews, C (1997) *The Essentials of Music Copying*, Music Publishers Association, London

Kingston, P (1993) *Working in Performing Arts* ('Working in' no. 90), Careers and Occupational Information Centre, Bristol

Lumley, J S P (1989) *The Art of Conducting*, Rhinegold, London

Sanger, D (1990) *Playing the Organ*, Novello, London

The UCAS Handbook, published annually, UCAS, Cheltenham

Watson, H and Throp, C (eds) *British and International Music Yearbook*, published annually, Rhinegold, London

Wright, D *The Complete Bandmaster*, Pergamon Press, Oxford

Fact sheets published by the Incorporated Society of Musicians, London

A Career in School Music Teaching

Approaching an Agent

Careers with Music

Music Therapy

The First Ten Years: Establishing a Solo Career

The First Two Years: Establishing an Orchestral Career

Newspapers and periodicals

Arts Business, BC Publications (fortnightly)

Brio, International Association of Music Libraries (twice annually)

Choir and Organ, Orpheus Publications (bi-monthly)

Church Times, G J Palmer & Sons (weekly – Friday)

Classical Music, Rhinegold (fortnightly)

The Daily Telegraph (daily)

Early Music Today, Rhinegold (bi-monthly)

The Guardian (daily)

The Independent (daily)

The Mix, 30 Monmouth Street, Bath BA1 2BW (four-weekly)

Museums and Arts Appointments, Rhinegold (fortnightly)

Music Journal, Incorporated Society of Musicians (monthly)

Music Scholar, Rhinegold (annually)

Music Teacher, Rhinegold (monthly)

Opera Now, Rhinegold (bi-monthly)

Das Orchester, Schott, Mainz (monthly); UK distributor: Interads International Media, Mayfayre House, 22–28 Shepherd Street, London W1Y 7LJ

Piano, Rhinegold (bi-monthly)

The Singer, Rhinegold (bi-monthly)

Sounding Board, Sound Sense (quarterly)

Studio Sound, 8 Montague Close, London Bridge, London SE1 9UR (monthly)

The Times Educational Supplement (weekly – Friday)

The Times Higher Educational Supplement (weekly – Friday)

Index

The Kogan Page *Careers in...* series

Visit Kogan Page on-line

Comprehensive information on
Kogan Page titles

Features include

- complete catalogue listings,
  including book reviews and
  descriptions

- special monthly promotions

- information on NEW titles and
  BESTSELLING titles

- a secure shopping basket facility
  for on-line ordering

PLUS everything you need to know
about KOGAN PAGE

http://www.kogan-page.co.uk